A Nav

The Struggle Within

By Rachel Pallitan

Disclaimer

This book is a product of the author's imagination. It springs from an actual life but it in no way gives any facts of that life. Everything written is fictitious. Names have been chosen at random from the author's own mind. The places are real but certain landmarks and descriptions have been changed and some settings may not exist. Names of come places have also been changed. Street names are made up. No living person is represented in this book. If any event holds true of any living person it is purely coincidental.

ISBN: 978-1-326-60874-3

Dedication

This book is dedicated to Jesus Christ, first and foremost. It is because of Him that I have written anything at all.

Secondly, I dedicate this book to all of my readers. Thank you for your interest in this subject and for your daring to read my first and what could be my only novel.

Acknowledgements

Photographs were taken while my father served in the Royal Navy and were his own property.

Introduction

How we feel on the inside is so often disregarded and even mocked in a condescending way, if we show it in public. If our behaviour is wayward as a result of such feelings, because of intense grief or other unsolved issues, people may come to the judge us as troublemakers or unsociable. Let's just put them into prison or drug them up or prescribe some other harsh treatment. Maybe not a physical prison but ostracizing us can make us feel that there is no escape from the turmoil within. We can also judge ourselves and become isolated and treat our closest with the worst of our behaviour. It is in the prisons where we often become introspective and come to terms with the downside of our humanity. Ralph Hopkins is one man who judged himself. Shame dominated his way of life until the day he died. When he reveals the reason behind who he had become through writing a journal, will his children shown him mercy or continue to condemn him?

Contents

Chapter One

He lay on his left side to relieve the congestion in his chest. Lung cancer had struck years before due to smoking cigarettes since he was a sixteen year old boy. His eldest daughter Beverly stared at his shriveled face and visible areas of skin on his hands and forearms. The side ward where he lay alone before she arrived looked and felt almost sterile. The typical hospital smell mingled with that of a dying person failed to impress her, though it was better than being in squalid conditions with more pungent aromas. She sat in the one chair provided and traced his laughter lines at the edge of his eyes where a trickle of a tear fell onto his pillow.

'Dad, please, forgive us for not understanding your life. You never told us. We never knew how hard it was for you. Now it is too late for you to say anything. I can only imagine that life did not give you a good innings.'

She held the oxygen mask up to his face so he could breathe and removed it again so that maybe he could say a few final words. He grimaced in pain, pain that speared his heart making him cough and grimace once more. After closing his eyes with the agony of coughing he opened them again and whispered to his daughter, Beverly – the stronger one of his children.

'There, there's a book in my...' he faltered. Not knowing whether or not he really should reveal his secrets, even at this stage, he closed his eyes and paused for a long time. Beverly squeezed his hand.

'It's okay, Dad. Try not to talk.'

He lifted his head slightly and, laying it down again, rested for a while before continuing in a laboured whisper, 'In the bookcase - you will find it right next to the Bible. Take it - and read it. Promise me that you will tell my story to the rest of the family; promise, promise to tell them that I love them, I always loved them.' He eased his weak grip on Beverly's hand. She rubbed his hand to warm it but it was not going to respond. She knew he would never wake up.

Beverly, being a nurse, closed his eyes gently and walked away. Her trance-like stare as she left the room and walked calmly towards the nurses station reflected the hollow life he had lived; the barrenness, the cruelty and disunity of a family rent in two by tragedy.

She left the ward deaf to the cries of needy patients in other side wards and yielded her father's care to the nurses in charge. She made her way directly to his home; the stone spattered one in the middle of a row of five terraced council houses, in Gillingham, Kent. A town she had never loved, simply because of the evil memories it held for her and her siblings. As she placed the key in the lock and turned it she wondered what she would find in that book. Making her way to his bedroom she pulled out the soft, brown leather journal. Its rugged edges showed it had lasted many decades. It slid out quite easily from beside the Bible. She pondered over what she would find in its pages and whether she should read it alone or call her sister, Paula and brothers, Carl and Sidney, to share first hand what their father had written about his life. What if she found something they ought not to know? She had been the only one at his bedside at his passing. The others were bound to be on their way when they found out it was possibly his last hour on earth. She wept as the remembrance of the man she never understood crossed her furrowed brow.

'Take it and read it. Promise me that you will tell my story to the rest of the family. Promise to let them know that I love them. I always loved them.'

The softness of the death bed meeting vanished from her mind. *How, how can he say he loved us? How can he say such things? Never was there a word to us that he ever loved us, never.*

She recalled the beatings, the rage, and the servitude of her and her siblings towards her father without even one word of gratitude and the sheer ignorance towards their young lives. Taking the book in her hands she scanned the front cover. The blur of tears obscured dark marks left on it by who knows what. A sudden knock at the front door startled her. She swallowed her tears before they fully emerged from a heart of deep regret, quickly hid the book in her bag and left it on the bed to collect later on. Determined not to say a word to anyone about it she raced downstairs and opened the door.

'Hi Beverly,' whispered Paula, breathlessly. 'We just got to the hospital but it was too late, he'd already died. I knew you would be here.'

Paula, a little calmer, turned and beckoned to Carl and Sidney who were waiting in Carl's blue mini for confirmation that Beverly had arrived. Carl nodded, switched off the engine and pulled on the hand brake. The brothers made their way down the short path to the front door, kicking through crisp, fallen leaves as they went. Beverly and Paula led them into the lounge where Beverly left to make a cup of tea in the kitchen. The cold tap juddered as she twisted it. A gush of water rattled the pipes under the sink as she filled the electric kettle. It boiled quicker than her swirling thoughts could make any sense of the news she had been given about the journal. Scooping three teaspoonfuls of tea into the large brown teapot she could not help thinking of the magnitude of work that needed to be done. She poured milk into the waiting mugs, filled each to the brim with the steaming tea and carried them steadily into the lounge. While handing them around she asked in quite a reserved tone, 'So, whose job is it to sort out the house? I guess all of ours but I am willing to sort it out myself if all of you are working flat out.'

Carl quickly glanced around the room before sipping the scalding tea and wondered what could be saved and what should be turfed out to charity shops. Their father was not exactly the richest of men by any means and so he agreed to let Beverly sort out the house. 'He hasn't made a will,' he guessed, 'because just look at what is left to us. Being a widower and a hermit, who took care of him?' He shook his head.

'He was unlivable with,' said Paula, 'he can't blame anyone for that.'

'Maybe he was blaming us,' Beverly suggested, 'people take stuff out of those nearest to them.'

'But why their own children?' answered Paula, somberly.

Sidney brushed a tear away while sitting deep in thought. Unable to answer Paula, who was training be a nurse and following in Beverly's footsteps, he forcefully pushed the enormity of pain down to the depths of his grieving soul, hiding the inner dam from the vision of his siblings. With his heavy, manly build nobody would guess how injured this 'little boy' of twenty seven really was.

Beverly ignored Paula's statement and question but by no means dismissed the impact it had on her. She said, while thinking about protecting the journal from being exposed, 'Okay, Carl, that settles things. Leave it to me.'

After being set aside in that way, Paula thought; *Beverly and Carl always called the shots*. Being the eldest, responsibility and leadership had left their indelible mark on them since they were small children. Paula turned to face Beverly, looking tired and offered help.

'You'll be busy studying, Paula, so no worries.'

'I can come in the afternoons on my days off. I'll have time then.'

Beverly rested her eyes and nodded; her thoughts still swirling. 'I'll take care of everything else too,' she offered. 'Thomas will not mind losing me for a bit while I get this sorted. He can look after himself. No good him being here, he hates this sort of thing; after death duties.'

Carl stood, stretched his arms upwards and yawned, 'I'll let you know when the funeral will be held. It should be in a few days. I informed Father O'Reilly from St Bede's about dad's death and will go round when I hear from him regarding the Requiem Mass and other funeral arrangements. You've no need to worry about that side of things, Beverly.'

'Thank you, Carl.' Beverly managed half a smile.

'We'll be off then. Let us know if you need us,' invited Carl.

He, Sidney and Paula left the house. Beverly stayed behind to get started. The sooner the clearing would be done, the better. She closed the door behind them only when they were well out of sight and both cars' engines could no longer be heard. Passing the lounge she glimpsed the time on the grandfather clock just prior to it chiming four. She had at least an hour to open up the journal and all the privacy she needed so slowly made her way back upstairs. Carl, Sidney and Paula would not be back for at least a week, she surmised.

Carl, older than Beverly by only a year and a half, carried an air of respect when dealing with formal matters. He had learned it as a mere boy of ten from his father after his mother's death. Now at the age of thirty he was an equally well respected Insurance Agent and demanded, or rather earned, respect from his wife, Dora and their only son, Joseph.

Beverly rummaged through her thoughts before sitting on the bed to open up the journal. Should she get started on the sorting or should she start reading? Should she, after all, wait and tell her siblings? No, it was too late now. If she tells them they will probably wonder why she had not said anything during tea when they were all together. Fearing the consequences that may ensue she slid it back next to the Bible. She would tell them anyway after she has read it. A breath of fresh air may help clear her perspective. She wandered downstairs, plucked her coat and bag from the peg and left the house. 'Cardboard boxes,' she said aloud and marched down the path, kicking the remaining leaves onto the sparse lawn on either side. She strode to the nearest newsagent to ask for the boxes. It was a fair walk and, after all, it would kill two birds with one stone, obtain boxes and get fresh air. Approaching the red pillar box ahead of her she wondered if the same man owned the shop beside it. Slowing her pace she opened the door. At the sound of the bell the shop owner appeared in the entrance from behind the blue ribbon screen. Brushing hands together he welcomed Beverly,

'Good afternoon,' he stopped abruptly, recognizing her. He only just greeted her when she introduced herself,

'Good afternoon, Mr Farlow? You are the Mr Farlow who owned the shop many years ago, aren't you? I'm Beverly Hopkins, you may not remember me.'

'Yes, I remember you. Didn't you have a sister and some brothers?'

'There were four of us and my father, Ralph.' She took a step backwards as he stepped forward to shake her hand. Quickly slipping his hand into his apron pocket, he smiled, a little embarrassed at the sudden reaction. Mr Farlow crept back behind the counter, addressing any further questions from there. He lowered his head before speaking again,

'I presume you are here to… I mean… I'm terribly sorry but last time I saw your father he was battling with his health. Are you visiting him?' he asked clumsily. Beverly softened her stance,

'No, he has passed away, Mr Farlow, just this week, two days ago to be precise. I'm sorting out his things.'

'He's passed away? How may I help?'

'Thank you. Yes, I am Beverly. I need as many boxes as possible, please, but I haven't brought my car and not much time, too much to think about. I can carry a couple if you have them but please put the rest aside. I'll have to come back with the car.'

'We have plenty out the back. I can sort them now while we are quiet and you can come and collect them.'

Mr Farlow disappeared through the screen. The swishing sound reminded Beverly of her childhood and how she used to run down there with Paula to buy their father's newspaper and hopefully be given a free blackjack chew.

Two huge boxes emerged first, hiding Mr Farlow's slight frame.

'There you are and mind how you go.'

'I'll be back right away.'

She left with her light burden of boxes and compared it with the burden she now carried. *Cruelty isn't obvious to the general public*, she thought, *but behind closed doors it can be as rampant as a bad cold.* After throwing the boxes into the house and closing the door a second time she drove back to the shop and filled her red Morris Minor to capacity with what remained of Mr Farlow's supplies. On returning to the house again she allocated boxes to particular rooms and left it at that for the day. In half an hour she would be home.

Not long after she arrived Carl phoned to let her know there would be a family funeral as their father was not well known. They discussed who should be invited. None of his brothers could be found in such a short space of time. If any still existed it would take many months to locate them. Father O'Reilly had arranged for the funeral to take place the following Thursday at ten thirty and would prepare what he could by whatever Carl thought his father would appreciate.

'I'm happy to leave all that with you, Carl. I'd better go.'

'Okay, Beverly, don't work too hard. See you on Thursday, bye.'

Thomas arrived home from work a quarter of an hour after Beverly. The thirty two year old medical consultant changed into his jeans, navy, polo neck jumper and trainers before starting to cook the supper. Even after a hard days work he loved taking his time preparing meals.

Beverly brought the kettle to the boil for their usual cup of tea and, while they drank and he cooked, she sat at the marble breakfast bar to explain about Carl's preparations for the funeral. Thomas left to forage for onions he had dug out of the garden in the summer, leaving her mid sentence. Their scent reached him before he even opened the door of the shed. On his return he half addressed Beverly, 'Look at these beauties.' While throwing the one in his left hand a couple of inches into the air and catching it, he added, 'Liver is no good without crisp, golden fried onions.' Peeling and chopping them without another word he listened to the rest of Beverly's explanation then with eyes watering profusely he cleared his throat to speak,

'I will probably not be able to attend, Beverly. I will be in an important meeting with other consultants but will get out of it if I can.'

Beverly shrugged sadly and watching him throw the chopped onions into the frying pan, she said, resignedly, 'It's an important time for me and the rest of us, Thomas, please try to be there.'

Thomas cleared his throat again. 'Look at me, Beverly; I said I would get out of it if I can.'

'Alright, it's just that I miss you at times like these.'

'It can't be helped,' he replied sharply.

Beverly hid her pain, 'I know.' she drank the last mouthful of her tea, left the kitchen, marched down the hall and then upstairs.

Thomas's best suit hung over the bedroom chair. She picked it up to hang in the wardrobe but noticing the creases at the back of the knees and front of the elbows and collecting her black funeral dress she returned to the kitchen and laid them on the spare stool until after the meal. Both ate in silence but the presence of stress left an unpleasant taste in their mouths.

Beverly slowly cleared away the plates for washing up after Thomas had disappeared with a mug of coffee to the lounge. When finished she remained in the kitchen, opened the door of the storage cupboard beside the sink and pulled out the ironing board.

'What are you doing?' Thomas's sudden arrival shocked her,

'Ironing my clothes for tomorrow and just in case you can make it I'm ironing yours too,' she answered while closing the cupboard door.

Without answering he left to change again but this time into his gym clothes. In what seemed to her like two minutes he was back. Staring at his muscles as he passed through, she thought, *he's not got many, but he tries.* Her face refused to smile. He turned abruptly, sensing her gaze penetrating his back. She turned away. He watched as she plugged in the iron and thought what a wonderful person she was. *Of only…* he thought, but I have set my boundaries. He hesitated and wondered if it was alright to give her a hug. No, he rounded the corner of the kitchen and ran down the steps to their home made gym.

On his return she had put away the ironing board, returned the clothes to the bedroom and had returned to the kitchen to clean the cupboards and clear out rubbish. He had had time to think while drinking his coffee about how well off he was. He would hate to lose it all on account of his charring attitude. To cast off Beverly would be like amputating a limb, a much needed limb. During his workout he mellowed more towards her and after reaching the kitchen when his time was up he merely stopped in the kitchen doorway to watch what she was doing. She was grieving, yes, but so was he, in a way. He had lost a father he never knew. She had lost a father she knew but never appreciated for whatever reason. He needed her hug right now. He cleared his throat loudly but remained where he was, slightly pouting. She carried on cleaning until he cleared his throat again.

'Are you alright?' she asked, suddenly giving him her full attention. She noted his shining low forehead with beads of sweat piercing his skin, his dilated pupils, letting in the brilliant light of the kitchen bulb and the pout. He heart softened as she made her way towards him. She slid the towel from around his neck and wiped his forehead with it. He reached out to retract the towel.

'No, actually I am feeling pretty sad about losing my dad. I know you have lost yours too but I never knew mine. I could do with a hug?'

She rested her head on his chest and wrapped her arms around his waist for a sweet moment but knowing it was only for him, just for him. If he knew what comfort she felt he would withdraw. To give was not on the menu, just to receive. She nestled a little longer and at that point he knew it was for her. Quickly he withdrew and left the kitchen. She folded the ironing board, lifted the cold iron from the breakfast counter and put them back where they belonged. As she had run the hot iron over the creases in his suit so she would run the creases out of their marriage before too long. Breaking the icy façade and winning him over would be accomplished one day. She could settle for his remote companionship but not his silent distance.

Thomas rose extra early the following morning, the day of the funeral, and left the house before his wife woke up. When Beverly woke to find him gone she felt the loneliness keenly but had practiced carrying disappointment almost all her life and so it was not new to her to have to walk through her day with yet another empty feeling. Once at the church she greeted her siblings. The coffin had been taken to a local Mortuary. The priest brought holy water and sprinkled it over the coffin reciting a few formal prayers before it was carried out and driven to the church. The family followed behind the hearse together in the mourner's car, all dressed in traditional mourners' clothes. The chief altar boy led them to their seats in the front row before returning to the Sacristy. A woman, also dressed in black, suddenly emerged from the rear of the church, briskly marched to the front, placed a bouquet of flowers on the coffin then briskly left. She looked neither right nor left. All the siblings turned as she disappeared through the doors. A stunned silence was all that remained of her presence until Carl gave a nod to the priest who appeared at the Sacristy door. He also wore black vestments out of choice to compliment the mourner's clothes. Father O'Reilly, followed by three altar boys, left and solemnly walked across the front of the church to begin the Requiem Mass. The bewildered family sat quietly and later listened as Father O'Reilly spoke of the last judgment in his carefully prepared sermon. Mr Hopkins would surely be judged for his sins if they had not been confessed and repented of and could have to spend a while in purgatory. It could be that God would have mercy on him yet, especially if his family prayed for him often, sprinkled holy water at his graveside or on the floor of the church or said the Rosary for his departed soul. He knew only too well what went on behind closed doors. The children's confessions had given him sound knowledge of that because of how it resulted in a few sins of their own. But what was it his business to interfere with the man and his choices? The Mass was there for all to know how they should behave. Confession should have been a turning point in any life but Mr Hopkins had not confessed any sins except for when he had missed Mass or confession. The shame of their father had not been addressed simply because it was not 'known' directly by the priest and what had been told to him in the confessional was totally confidential. A fear of their Creator filled their hearts.

After the closing hymn and Father O'Reilly had sprinkled the coffin with holy water and waved the incense the siblings left with faces to the ground but not until the six pallbearers slowly lifted the coffin onto their broad shoulders and made their way out down the aisle and towards the open doors. The driver of the hearse marched slowly before them.

At the graveside there was no sign of Thomas so Beverly held on to Carl, Sidney and Paula in turn. They too needed comfort and she would not allow them to go without on account of her own rejection. After the burial they were driven back to Carl's house in the funeral car they had come in. Dora, who had not attended the funeral, on account of Joseph being too young, had prepared a wake. As they sat talking but not finding much to say Carl stood, announcing that somebody was standing outside the front door. Carl quickly reached the door before the doorbell rang. Everyone fell silent as Thomas put on an air of respect before entering the lounge. He glanced around the room, greeted them with a quick hello and sat beside Beverly.

'Can we leave now,' he whispered.

'What?'

'I need to get home. I managed to get some time off but I have to go home and return to work after lunch.'

'You can join us for lunch here, there is plenty.'

'Well, if you are sure it is no trouble.' He turned quickly for Carl's approval.

'You can help yourself, Thomas,' offered Carl, 'make yourself at home.'

Thomas smiled wryly. He had played his part well without a trace of guilt. If they had noticed anything they certainly didn't show it.

'I'll bring Beverly home later,' said Carl.

So Thomas ate then left just as easily as he had entered.

After Beverly's day off she returned to her father's house to continue cleaning. She had almost finished clearing the downstairs. Nothing important there had raised its head, just as she expected. Paula should be contacting her about now, she thought, and the phone rang as the thought dismissed itself.

'Hi, it's Paula, Beverly; I'm ready to come over to help now?'

'Hi, that's great, I've finished the downstairs. There wasn't much of value to sort out there. I've kept some things like old Navy records and medals, things like that for family sake and for any generations beyond us, like Carl's child; not sure if he will be interested or not.'

'Would you like me to bring anything?'

'No, just yourself. I have plenty of boxes. We can start in dad's ...' she coughed, remembering the journal she had put aside. Not that she had forgotten but during the engrossed concentration of the past week she had put it way to the back of her mind.

'Start the, kitchen?'

'No, um, that's already done, the upstairs bedrooms. It won't take long now.' She spoke calmly so as not to arouse suspicion.

'See you soon then.'

'Yes, bye.'

After putting the phone down Beverly raced upstairs, took the journal from what had been its safest place so far and opened it. She waited for Paula without starting on the bedrooms. With no time for a cup of tea until Paula arrived she turned to the back page. It was blank. Ah, so she turned the pages from the back until she found on the third to last page, the final entry of her father; the last words he had spoken to her on his deathbed: 'To whoever finds this journal, please promise me that you will tell my story to the rest of the family; promise, promise to tell them that I love them, I always loved them.'

Loved us? She turned to the back of the page and only just read the final paragraph when the door bell rang. Her face paled before placing the book back where it came from. With her spirit confused she walked slowly down the stairs and let Paula in.

'Hi, how's it going?' Paula asked while wiping her feet on the worn out and filthy door mat.

'As I said, I've finished downstairs. Let's have a cup of tea first then we can discuss what to do next.'

'You look rather pale, are you alright?' Paula hung her coat and scarf on the wall mounted rack.

'No, um, yes.' Beverly detached her inner thoughts from Paula as they made their way to the kitchen, and put the kettle on to boil.

'Are you sure you are alright? Has something happened since we last met?'

'No, err, yes. I mean… Let's get our tea and sit in the lounge. I have something to tell you.'

Once comfortable in the lounge and Paula had sat to attention, Beverly told her the final words of her father.

'Loved us? What do you mean?' asked Paula while lifting her mug.

'He was serious. People are always serious on their deathbeds.'

'How then, how did he love us? He never said he did and he certainly didn't act one bit like he loved us, except Sidney once in a while.' Paula placed her mug on the coffee table and faced Beverly.

'I always kind of knew there was something wrong with him, something bothering him. But, no, he never said a word. But he did…' Beverly coughed and swallowed her words, waving her right hand in front of her mouth.

'Did what?'

'Did say something else but it's not important really.'

'On his deathbed, what? It must have been important.' Paula pressed.

'If I tell you, you must keep it to yourself. Never tell our brothers what else he said. I don't think I can do this alone.'

'What alone?'

'Nothing.'

'It's not nothing, it's something. Now you've told me so much. If I don't know what you're hinting at, I'll probably have to ask Carl and Sidney what it could be.' Paula lifted her mug to her drying lips. Her eyes darted warily towards her sister.

'Promise me first that if I tell you, you will not mention it to them until we both know exactly.'

'Know what?' Paula glanced out of the window. 'Alright, I promise I won't mention it.'

'No matter what?'

'Yes, I won't mention it.'

'Okay, we must keep it to ourselves until we have finished reading it.'

'Reading what?'

'It's a book. A book dad wrote. Well, not a book, a journal. I just read the last page, well, what was on that page was what he said on his deathbed but in the next to last entry he said something else but we must read it from the beginning together. I don't want to read it alone, Paula, and you wouldn't want to either. After that we must decide how to tell Carl and Sidney.' Holding her empty mug in her hands Beverly concentrated her eyes on Paula's expression.

'Where is it, the book?'

'Drink your tea and then I'll take you to it.'

Paula gulped the final mouthful, rested the mug back on the table and lowered her eyelids. Beverly took note of the appearance of fear as it crossed her sister's face and the deepening frown whose lines distorted the smooth skin of her forehead. Leaving her mug on the table Beverly took two steps towards Paula and slightly bent to pat her on the shoulder. It was not the time to divulge good or bad information. Paula stood, straightened her skirt with a sweeping movement and allowed Beverly to lead the way out of the room and on upstairs to their father's bedroom. Reaching once more for the journal she invited Paula to sit on the bed, 'Why sit on the bed? Let's take it downstairs where we will be more comfortable,' suggested Paula.

'I'd rather we sit here. I have a dreadful fear of losing it if I take it outside of this room. When we have finished, however much we get through at any one time, it will go straight back in the bookcase where its home is and will be until the house is empty.'

'That won't be too long from now, will it? Then you will take it home with you, I guess.'

'No, err, yes. No, it won't be too long from now.'

Beverly opened the journal from the front, as what she had already seen written on that back page, causing her face to grow pale, was not to be read again until reaching that page the proper way.

'It's quite a thick book,' observed Paula.

'Yes, we will read so much and then sort out our old room, then read some more and then sort out the boys' old room and so on. Dad never did a thing to ever sort anything out, even after we had all left.'

'He didn't care.'

'Never mind, we'll find out what he never told us right here and he isn't here so whatever it brings up for us he has well and truly escaped from. I'll read it out loud this time and you can next time if you want, but we must read it together, one of us out loud and the other silently. Here we go then, you ready?'

Sitting beside Beverly with her head inclined towards the page Paula, saluting, said, 'Ready.'

With both pairs of eyes alert and her mouth ready for the first words, Beverly cleared her throat and began, 'Dated Thursday, June 15th 1967 "I always wanted to write, having been given this journal as a gift for my twenty first birthday but never had the opportunity. Now I do. Boys don't cry, do they? Since I was a small boy, I never cried; only the hint of a tear when my father died. I was only five years old; that was 1917. Five, and told not to cry with the back hand of my mother. This journal is the story of my life as far back as I can remember; of course, not all of it, just flashbacks here and there. I want my children to know me – when I'm gone. How can I tell them face to face? They were only small and had lost their mother to an incurable illness. I write of the nineteen forties. I cannot cry, remembering the pain of that grief I tried to let out only the day before my father died and the additional pain of my mother's rough hand. She worked hard, my mother; a well built woman and not to be trifled with. She always had her hair in a bun and an apron around her waist. When my father died, she changed. I am one of her eight sons. None of us talk to each other now because we were all separated just after his death. It's as though she didn't want to be reminded of her marriage. We were sent to different children's homes the day she took off her apron and never put it back on. At least I never

20

saw it back on because I never saw her again. As for my brothers and me we didn't know how to contact each other, that's why we don't talk to each other. I could not get out of anyone where they were. In those days they didn't tell children anything and this day also I will tell nothing except what I write here in this journal. Neither did they care about how we felt. I loved my brothers, all of them, deeply. We were sent off all on the same day, perhaps because it was easier that way but I have no idea what day of the year it was. I recall the faces of my brothers from fifteen year old Edwin to three year old Stephen when told only that morning that they were going to live somewhere else. Even the twins Arthur and James were separated that day. It was all so quick. One minute they seemed relaxed and the next crying, all of them and me? I held on to any tear trying to find its way to the surface of my eyes. My mother turned her back the minute the care authorities took the boys and disappeared into the house. That, by far, was the most dreadful day of my life. Torn from my father and torn from my family in just one short week. Torn from my own mother and torn inside, confused.

The journey away from my home that day is a vague memory but I do remember sitting on a rugged seat in a kind of truck. There were other boys about my age too, about six of us and I stared at each of them in turn. They stared back. Some were crying, some with glazed expressions. All were poor and ragged. I closed my eyes, controlling the welling-up, crossed my legs and then after opening my dry eyes stared at the floor of the truck and waited for it to stop. After what seemed like hours, it did, and I needed the toilet, had to hold on with that too.

My wife died in 1943 and I sit here on my bed still unable to cry even half a tear wondering why I alienated my own four children, why I beat them so cruelly and ignored their growing up years. Why did I not prepare them for what lay ahead in their lives? I am about to say why but I need to ask myself why so that I can answer anyone questioning the very same thing.

I should never have given up on the Navy. After the births of Carl and Beverly, Emma, my wife, wanted me to leave. She insisted that I be with them and serve as a father, to relinquish my newly acquired Petty Officer status. She had missed out on her own parents, having also lived in an orphanage, so knew the importance of having them around. She wanted a family life, a happy family life. I did not want to be around. I loved the sea and I loved… 'her,' at first anyway. Not Emma, though I did love her, I married her. I loved Emma but it was her, not Emma where my chief loyalties had to lie; had to. How can I bring myself to write about 'her?' This is a private book and will not be shared with anyone until I release it, when I'm gone. They, my children, will never know there was a 'her,' or a him. Yes, him, her son. The one she dragged out of me one night on HMS Terrible. I call it Terrible, though that was not its name. How can I associate that ship with what happened on board the night that… 'her.' She will never see this book. NEVER!'"

Beverly breathed deeply and placed her hand firmly on the page. Paula did not look up.

'Let's do something else for a bit.' Beverly suggested, 'I need space to think.'

'Okay,' was all Paula could manage.

Beverly closed the journal and, in dazed bewilderment, left the room. Paula remained for a few minutes trying to gather her thoughts then followed Beverly but not before she noticed the journal had been left on the bed. Quickly leafing through to the final entry she removed it hastily. Placing it in her bag she loudly and nonchalantly declared,

'We have a half brother!'

'I know. I just can't drum up any feelings having read that. You see, we cannot read that journal alone. What will we find next? And who was, 'her'?'

'Do you think we ought to try and find him, this brother, and do you think we should tell Carl and Sidney?'

'I can't think about that right now. I need a break for a while to get used to the shock,' called Beverly from the bathroom.

'Okay, I'll go and put the journal back next to the Bible for you, then come and help. We can discuss it later.' A sense of wry satisfaction pervaded Paula's heart. Beverly is not the one in charge now, she thought. 'Where are you starting? I'll have to leave after we've read the next bit, got to study for my exam.'

Beverly emerged from the bathroom and met Paula along the landing. 'Let's start in the boys room so we can finish with ours last. It will take a good week to sort stuff, read and clean. By that time we should at least be half way through the journal. Oh, of course, you can only help today. When is your next day off?'

'I have a couple of days off at the end of next week,' Paula said while pulling the bedroom curtain across, 'We have to draw all the curtains, don't we. Isn't that what people do when somebody has died? I'll come back then and we can read a good lot of it. I really want to finish it so we can get to that last page you mentioned and turned pale over.'

'Leave the curtain, we need the light. Anyway, I think they only draw them when the coffin is in the house, don't they? Please don't look at that last page. We need to get to that part together.'

Paula turned her lips sideways as if pouting to the right while facing the bare window. An enormous feeling of guilt made her cough. She twirled her shoulder length hair round her right forefinger before turning back to Beverly,

'Okay, I won't look.'

Paula had never been in charge and found herself in a sticky position. She would have to leave the page in her bag. How would she put it back? The journal now damaged because of its removal.

'Let's get started then. Give ourselves a rest from that.' Beverly ordered gently.

After at least an hour sorting out old clothes, a few books and a couple of games, they stripped the beds. 'Remember sleeping on these? How uncomfortable with the springs poking through the one inch mattresses. He must have nicked them from HMS Terrible.

'He must have,' laughed Paula.

'I simply cannot understand dad not clearing all this out for such a long time.'

'We'll roll up this rug then go for a snack and a cup of tea. We can forget any further reading if you like today. I still need time to adjust to her and her son. How about you? Didn't you feel shocked?'

'I think we need to find her son.'

'What good would that do? I'll put this on the landing,' Beverly carried the rug out.

'Just a thought, it's up to you. Maybe we can read a little more before I go? I'd like to read my bit today if that's okay with you and then we would both have read some.'

After they enjoyed the most welcome toasted crumpets and tea they took to the stairs again but this time Paula left her bag in the lounge, just in case she opened it by mistake in front of Beverly. Beverly took the journal from the shelf and handed it to Paula who opened it. One of the front pages came loose in her hand. The one that corresponded to the back page she had removed. There was stunned silence for a few seconds.

'What?' Beverly asked, 'Why has that happened? Give it to me.'

'Maybe it was already loose, Beverly, and you just didn't notice.'

'Maybe it was. I'm tired with all this grief, stress and sudden surprises.'

'Let's leave it then. I don't mind reading the next bit when I come back.' Paula did not want to be found out.

'We'll have to be careful how we handle it. We don't want to lose any pages, Paula. While you are away I will make sure there are no more loose ones and I better number them in pencil in case any fall out. Dad wants us to know his story and we must read it all, not to have pages missing.'

'Good idea, we can't be having that either.'

'No.'

Paula saw her chance in maintaining innocence. Perhaps Beverly will accidentally 'lose' the back page or at least she could convince her that she did. Just to get off the hook if she found out tonight. She would not be able to persuade Beverly it wasn't her.

'I think you should read your bit now and then it's evens. You don't have to read much if you don't want to.'

Paula agreed, 'Okay, I'll just read a bit.' She did not want to get through the book at all now. No matter about the back page. Ah, she could put it back, of course and suggest it was loose seen as the front one was already. So that was it, the next chance she got she would put it back and breathe a sigh of relief. She could not do that now as she had left her bag downstairs and Beverly was sitting right there.

'Beverly, will you leave the work till I get back next week? Take a break and then we can work together, how about that?'

'I need to get it done really but, alright, two hands are better than one. Let's both come back then, when you are off.'

'I'll get reading my bit now then we can go home.' Paula turned the pages carefully faking her concern. She knew no more pages would be loose but just in case and to appear innocent, she moved her hands slowly. 'You ready?'

'Yes,' sighed Beverly.

'I'll read to the next entry, it's not much. Then we will know where we are up to each time if we do it like that. So where were we? He would never let – 'her'- read it. "Date, Wednesday, 20th September, 1967. I have lost it all. Losing things you hold dear and when you expect them to be as certain as the air you breathe, is far more devastating than having a mere dream and losing that, when you have not built anything from that dream, as long as you are in your heart knowing it is just a dream. When Emma insisted on my leaving the Navy I felt wanted for the first time in my life. Yes, I was torn with my decision. After all I had been in the Navy for twelve years and only just been promoted. I could have stayed because she is now gone; left me with nothing but heartache and memories and… 'her' and her boy. Yes, I had my own children but what were they without a mother and with a broken father? I could not introduce… her to them. She was, and is, far from an ideal woman and to expect her to love my children, Emma's children, would be asking far too much and she would not anyway; she hated and still hates them. Oh, how she loved her son, wanted everything for him, even the crown if she could get it. I could have stood my ground, if only I knew then that it would all turn out this way. Life on land does not allow a person to look out to the horizon to see if anything lies beyond it. I am all at sea, even here, without a ship, all at sea in the turbulence of my thoughts. Without a horizon there is no hope.'

Paula stopped reading, rubbed her eyes and lay the book down on her lap.

'There,' she sighed, 'that's my entry finished. I'll put it back.'

In total silence they proceeded from the room which held no good memories for either of them. The three foot single bed with its crimson eiderdown caressed Paula's fingertips as she stood, slightly bent, concealing the burden she carried. No matter, it would not be for long. She shrugged. After checking around the house that all was reasonably alright to leave for a week, Beverly linked Paula's arm and they both wandered down the creaky, thread bare, beige carpeted stairs and out through the front door which automatically locked behind them when pulling it to.

Paula waved Beverly off as she drove away before strolling pensively towards her own car. She pulled her car keys, which she always carried separately from her bag, from her pocket, unlocked the door to climb in and started the ignition. She waited a few moments before driving away in a dream. As she passed a local pub she decided on having a meal. Parking in the only space left she made her way past strategically placed shrubs in their containers showing off brilliant white flowers, through the small wooden door and to the counter to order. Suddenly realizing she had left the house without her bag she quickly turned about to leave and hurried outside. Thoughts raced, adrenaline pumped. How could she contact Beverly? Without a phone box in sight and, in any case, unable to remember her number off by heart, she had only one thing to do, back out of the bay and drive home. The bag should be fine for a week where it was. There was nothing in it that was of great importance, except that of the last page of the journal and a ten pound note with some small change in a little purse. She would have to make do with anything she needed, in the meantime, by using spares and carrying her main purse around for the week. Forcing herself to push the bag out of her mind she arrived home regretting that she now had to cook her own meal and worrying, albeit unwillingly, about that last page.

Chapter Two

Carl woke up from a deep sleep the morning after his sisters' reading. He drifted in and out of grief; not knowing whether to cry or remain slightly aloof from the process of losing anyone, let alone his father. He was used to being in charge and wondered how Beverly was managing with sorting things out. He would pay her a visit at the terraced council house they had lived in all their lives until their father ushered them away as soon as they reached sixteen. He didn't like the house but was fond of his sister, both of his sisters. Maybe Beverly had finished the sorting by now and he did not want to keep disturbing her but could not shake off the fact that the responsibility should first land on his shoulders, being the eldest. Saturday, tomorrow, he would go along, take his key and surprise her by offering his help.

After work that evening he pulled up in the wide driveway that led to his own abode; a far cry from the shabby old joint they once called home. With shoes so brilliantly shined by his six year old son, he stepped from the car. Joseph, a lively little fair haired lad, loved to be around his father and offered a helping hand whenever he could. His grandfather had taught him how to clean shoes as only an expert Navy lad could. Dora, who Carl had met and later married at the Catholic Church, opened the front door as soon as she heard the engine switch off. Joseph stood beside her grinning and shouted,

'Hello, Daddy.'

After a brief but hearty, 'hello', Carl sped upstairs to change clothes. Before dinner he told Dora of his plans for the following day.

'You will be alright looking after Joseph, will you? It will be a fine sunny day and you could take him to the playground in the big park.'

Dora smiled while dishing out the spaghetti Bolognese on their everyday plates. 'Anything you say, boss. Beverly should be happy of some help.'

'It's one thing helping. It's another taking orders from Beverly. It's usually the other way around. Some humility on my part will be necessary, I reckon, but she's a great organizer so no real worries.'

'Let's have a twosome evening after Joseph is in bed. You can catch me up on a few things. We haven't had much quality time for a bit,' Dora suggested as she flicked her hanging fringe out of the way with a toss of her head.

'We're always having quality time, aren't we Joseph?' Carl addressed his son while reaching for his dinner, 'there you are. Now you eat up and don't leave anything.'

Dora watched how tenderly Carl lowered the plate. Her son sure was handsome with those dimples!

'There's nothing but good reports from school,' she said, 'and he's going to be part of the Christmas play, aren't you? Why did they choose you?'

'Because my name's Joseph and I look like him. Daddy do you think Joseph ate sketty bollinaise? Can you cut the sketty for me? But leave one long one so I can suck it up.'

'You are not sucking it up; it will fly all over your face if you do.'

'I like it doing that.'

'No, you will have bits of meat and stuff splattering over the walls, the ceiling and everywhere; definitely not. We can have a game of snakes and ladders after the washing up is done and then it's bed, okay?'

'Okay.'

Dora handed Carl his dinner then dished up her own. The three of them huddled around the saucepans and bowl of grated cheese she had placed on the table.

'Mummy says I can have a dog if you let me,' announced Joseph, 'he will like the bolly part but not the sketty.'

'Did you Mummy? Maybe for your birthday in January but you will have to look after him and no giving him any bolly. He has to have proper dog food, like you have to have proper human food.'

When they finished eating and clearing away Carl carried Joseph into the lounge for the promised game, tossing him over his shoulder as they went. Dora followed and sat watching before taking her knitting from her knitting bag.

'That's for me,' said Joseph pointing in Dora's direction. His small hands reached for the dice and he was sure to win if Carl had anything to do with it. Carl threw the dice quite hard so that it fell on the floor and if a six appeared he scooped it up and threw it again until he got a one or two. Joseph followed suit and threw it until it landed on a five or six.

'Isn't it time for bed yet?' asked Dora after only finishing four rows and while they were having so much fun laughing.

'No,' teased Joseph.

'No,' echoed Carl, 'this is far too important, what do you say Joseph?' He reached out to tickle his son. Dora wanted to block her ears as the joy and laughter reached crisis point. Crisis for her that is, not them. She laid her knitting on the floor, waltzed out of the room and fled upstairs to the bathroom. Turning on the taps, balancing the temperature, she made sure the bath was not going to be too hot for Joseph.

'Carl,' she shouted, 'Carl! Bring Joseph up for his bath and no more playing.'

There was no response from downstairs. She turned the taps off and returned to the lounge, 'Just look at you two; time for bed Joseph. Daddy will bath you then read you a story.' Father and son looked quite content sitting on the settee together after the hard playing. Carl removed his arm from around Joseph, took his hand and led him to the bottom of the stairs where he crouched down,

'Hop on, Piggy,'

Dora stood with her hands on her hips. The two of them were in a world of their own when together. It'll soon be my world with Carl; she thought and sat down to resume her knitting.

Dora looked forward to her times with Carl. Evenings were the only time when she could discover his plans for the days or weeks ahead and maybe a little more about him. Half an hour passed when Dora heard the, "Goodnight Joseph" Carl always uttered when leaving his son to get to sleep or maybe when he was already asleep. Her heart beat a little faster as he entered the lounge.

'Would you like a cup of coffee? I'm making one for myself,' offered Carl.

'That would be most welcome,' Dora said while finishing her row. She waited until the coffee arrived, patted the cushion and invited Carl to sit beside her. 'Look at the time already, half past eight,'

'I know but he needs his time with me. Don't I know what it's like to be without a father who loves me? I want him to remember me for good and not for bad.' He added two teaspoonfuls of brown sugar to his coffee then offered Dora the bowl. 'Oh, I'm sorry I should have given that to you first.'

'No problem.' She stirred in her sugar and made sure he stirred his thoroughly too. 'So what are we going to talk about tonight? How are you getting on with Beverly?'

'Just fine, there's not much to report but as I mentioned I'm going to play my part tomorrow so I'm wanting an early night. I need to put that game away.'

'I'll do that tomorrow. Tell me, how was your relationship with your father?' Dora reached out for his hand after taking a sip of coffee and replacing her mug on the tray. Replacing his too he sat back, leaned his head back against the couch and let his mind wander back to the six year old lad his son was now. He closed his eyes trying to visualize his father, then his mother. Dora waited. She knew he would open up eventually. He took comfort in her gently stroking his hand. Flashes of his father addressing his mother sharply one time fuelled pain in his chest. He watched his mother washing socks with a bar of soap then handing a sock to him and teaching him how to get them clean. For a young lad he did quite well but she always had to wash them after him to get them really clean. *But this isn't what Dora is asking*, he thought, she wants to know my relationship with my father. He kept his eyes closed.

'It's okay, take your time,' his psychologist wife was not going to push the issue. His memories had to come when he was well and truly relaxed, and they would come, for her.

He knew why she asked such questions. She had already explained that opening up was the best way in for healing to come and this would be a time for him to receive the free therapy.

'Dora, I can't remember dad loving me the way I love Joseph. How come I can love him the way I do when I have never experienced anything myself?' His hand began to sweat so he removed it from hers and pushed it along his trouser leg to get most of the moisture off. She took it up again. He carried on, 'It was, he was in the Navy, then he came back and lived with us but he wasn't happy. I would look at him and wonder why he shouted at mum sometimes. I can't remember his saying much to me until after mum died. Of course she was with him quite a bit before that and she understood him, must have. The only thing I would say is that the time he spent with me was when he gave directions and asking me to do stuff all the time. I remember Beverly coming up to him one day, after mum died, she must have been about eight and I must have been about nine and a half or ten. She hadn't done one of her jobs properly. Dad stood with the broom and made her sweep the entire back garden path until not a weed remained in the cracks. He wouldn't let me help but she couldn't get all the weeds up. She was only a child. He got so angry that day that he beat her with that broom; whacked her across the legs with it so hard that I cried, then he went for me and told me I would be a soldier one day and that I should not cry but be tough. He told me I would have to do that to the soldiers who didn't do their work. He said he didn't want me to ever join the Navy unless there was no room in the Army. That's what he said, I remember now. I looked into his eyes that day, they were icy blue and penetrated me like icicles but I kind of felt warm too. I wanted to help Beverly but he wouldn't let me. I loved him, Dora, all children love their parents and I wanted him to love him, maybe that's why I felt warm.' Dora lifted his hand to her heart. He felt it beating then he reached towards her.

'That's it,' she said, 'you can feel my love for you. Now what about Beverly? How is she getting on with the house?'

'She is wonderful, dad made a good job out of us in that respect but her heart is empty and I know, by mere observation, that she longs for a touch from Thomas but he isn't responding to her at all. He seems so distant.'

Dora smiled but Carl was not aware of that smile; his head resting on her shoulder hid it from view.

'When you come back from the house tomorrow we can have another time like this together and you can tell me everything that went on; how it affected you and things like that. It may well trigger a lot. You will need the time and I will give you all the time I have to spare.'

'You are marvelous, Dora, I love you very much. You and Joseph mean the world to me. I would not be able to get by without you.'

'Let's get to bed now then you will be refreshed for the morning. I'll take Joseph to the park as you suggested.'

Nicely relaxed, Dora left Carl, to make a hot chocolate in the kitchen. This time he waited for her return. He closed his eyes and drifted into a semi sleep. He tried to imagine taking his father's hand on the ships he sailed in but it was difficult. His father remained absent but Dora promised never to leave him in a place of sorrow. It was at those times that he spoke to her the most. Sitting beside him meant he didn't have to give eye contact and seeing a specialist counselor always entailed doing just that. He was ready for his hot chocolate when it arrived. Dora carried both mugs up to the bedroom where they drank quietly before retiring for the night. After their tranquil sleep they woke as the dawn chorus approached its end. What a wonderful symphony of birdsong to start the day, Carl thought.

On arriving at the house later in the morning images of his father flashed through his mind again; flashbacks of brutality, rage and dismissal of the slightest request. *If only*, he thought, *it would have been different*. Could he have changed it, done something about the attitude of his father? He had done his very best to serve him well. No ideas presented themselves, he had wrung himself out with good deeds and still it was not enough to placate the behaviour of the one who should have been the greatest hero of his life. He brushed all these thoughts aside and suppressed his own anger. Determining that Joseph would not suffer in the same way he removed his keys from the ignition, wandered down the path and unlocked the front door. He pushed it open before shouting, 'Hi, Beverly! Beverly!'

He took a quick look downstairs, picked up Paula's bag which he assumed belonged to Beverly and then dashed up the stairs two by two.

'Beverly?'

He stood pondering why Beverly was not around. After entering his father's bedroom he laid Paula's bag on the bed. Perhaps Beverly would turn up in a bit to collect her bag. He wondered about sorting a few things out without her. It should, after all, be the son's job to sort out the father's room. He ambled over to the window and looked outside. Thoughts of his father returned, flashing past the window then fading to make the garden appear duller than ever. He abruptly turned to scan the room for a second and puzzled over where to start. Deciding it would be best to empty whatever the furniture held inside he opened first the bedside locker drawer. The clutter that met his eyes mesmerized him; jars of vapour rub, a key ring, a comb, two more combs hiding at the back underneath a neatly ironed handkerchief. Having to think about what to do with such small objects caused him to change his mind. Was it the son's job to sort the room out after all? He sat for a while on the bed before resting his hand behind him. Lowering himself he lay back for a few minutes and thought how fortunate he was to have a beautiful wife and well cared for son. He *would* help Beverly and so raised himself up again. Returning to the drawer and emptying the contents onto the bed he found a small piece of torn off paper which had been folded in half. Almost absentmindedly he opened it and read what his father had written. He knew his father's hand writing as he had seen so many times the neat way his y's were written with the tail being double backed and the i's always dotted after the actual letter. 'I want this woman out of my life,' it read. Woman? What woman? His mother? His face grimaced as his mind became confused… he couldn't have, have, killed her? No, it was tuberculosis that killed her but what if it wasn't? What if…? He grabbed Paula's bag, ran downstairs, slammed the door behind him and left for Beverly's. Careful not to break the speed limit, he drove at the maximum speed allowed, reaching her house feeling cold and clammy.

The rapid knocking startled her as she dozed in her favourite recliner in the lounge after some heavy gardening with Thomas.

'I'll get it,' shouted Thomas from the kitchen.

Carl's wide brown eyes and flushed face pushed their way towards Thomas's perplexed expression.

'Is Beverly here?'

'Of course, but what…? Come in.'

Carl was already inside before the invitation. He raced past the full length hall mirror without taking his usual glance and screeched to a halt as Beverly appeared from her slumber. With her hair ruffled and the odd trace of a fallen leaf, revealing that she had been apple picking, she ran her hands down her jeans as though straightening a much loved skirt.

'I'm so sorry Beverly,' his urgent voice whispered, 'but I've something to tell you. Let's go somewhere where we can both sit down.'

'What is it?' She asked with a concerned expression as she led Carl, followed by Thomas, to the kitchen. Each sat half on and half off the high wooden breakfast stools. Breakfast had long been consumed. Beverly nervously took one of the washed apples from the cut crystal fruit bowl. Carl pushed her hand back towards the bowl. She gently dropped the apple and gave him her full attention. Thomas sat beside her. Carl unapologetically addressed him,

'Thomas, this is about our dad. I need to speak to Beverly alone.'

'No,' said Beverly, 'it's okay. We don't have secrets.'

'Maybe you can tell him later. I need to talk to you alone. Nothing personal, Thomas, you understand, just something private for now. If Beverly thinks you would benefit from hearing this she can tell you later.'

Thomas pouted and wandered back into the garden alone but stopped short of being totally out of earshot. Carl, using his peripheral vision, took note and so kept his voice down and offered his back to Thomas's view should he turn fully towards them.

'Beverly, I've just been to dad's house. You weren't there. I decided to help after all. I thought the whole thing over last night and came to the conclusion you shouldn't be given all the responsibility. But I saw you have done so much already. Have you found anything of interest?'

'What do you mean?'

'I mean, I was just about to start helping by sorting dad's stuff out, well, I did start, then changed my mind but changed it again. I found this.' He noticed her swallow sharply and grow pale. Putting his hand in his jacket pocket he pulled out the small piece of paper.

'What is it?' she managed, almost incoherently. Her colour returned when she saw its size, that it wasn't the journal.

'I think dad killed mum,' he said, suddenly shaking. 'Read this.'

She took the paper, read it, and with barely time to think, let alone fully awaken from her doze, asked,

'He did?'

'He definitely wanted her out of his life. It's his handwriting. Our mother, Beverly, murdered. The thought never crossed my mind but having said that, he did seem the type of man to do something like that. He often stopped short of losing it with us and at times we were so scared of him that we wondered if we would still be alive the following day.'

Beverly allowed her hand to wander over to the apple again. Carl stopped her a second time. She needed time to think, really think.

'Mum, murdered? I don't think he would. He was probably just angry at the time but I doubt if he would actually get rid of her, he loved her. He did seem a bit shifty at times and especially around her. Even as a child I noticed that, but to murder her, I don't think so. He only became violent *after* she died.'

'He did give her a hard time.'

'Not all the time.'

'We will have to find her death certificate to determine the cause of her death. Then we'll know for sure if she really did die of tuberculosis. Also, Beverly, here's your bag. You left it behind.'

She received the bag quietly and nonchalantly.

'That's Paula's bag, she obviously forgot it. We took a break since she last came to help because… and decided to do the rest of the sorting together. I would keep calm if I were you and wait till we can find the death certificate. Paula and I should find it when we get back.'

'No, we ought to go right now and try to find it. I won't be able to sleep till I find out what happened to her. We may have to call the police and if there is a time lag we could be arrested for covering up.'

'Okay, I'll have a word with Thomas.'

'Don't tell him why, Beverly. Not until we know for sure.'

She dismounted from the stool. Carl watched as she approached Thomas in the greenhouse. As far as he could make out the exchange of conversation had brought a positive outcome.

She announced on re-entering the kitchen 'It's okay, I managed to persuade him.' Wiping her feet on the door mat and looking behind her through the window towards Thomas she added, 'and he's happy to get some space in the garden.'

They left the kitchen. Reaching for their coats in the hall they hurried through the front door. Carl drove the half hour journey from Sittingbourne to Gillingham in silence, both of them in their own worlds. Paula's bag sat lazily on Beverly's lap. She would put it back where Carl found it and then make sure he did not venture too close to the journal. Once upstairs Carl showed Beverly the drawer where he found the paper.

'Do you realize that your fingerprints are all over that paper now, Carl? So going to the police may not be an option.'

Carl ignored the comment which made him all the more determined to find the certificate, or should he forget it? But it was definitely his father's handwriting so he shrugged it off.

'You search the rest of the locker and I'll search the library,' stated Beverly.

'Fair enough.'

Carl wondered where his father would have put all his important papers as he made his way back to the bedside locker. He returned what he had removed earlier to the drawer then, after opening the cupboard door, pulled the contents out in two handfuls, dumping them on the bed. Fumbling through bits of tissue, once sodden and screwed up, he found a large brown envelope. Why so many tissues? But again he dismissed thinking too much. He opened the envelope while glancing quickly towards Beverly. He stopped to watch as she caressed the slightly protruding spine of what looked like a brown, tatty book.

'You found something, Beverly?' she shoved the book back into its place. Quickly turning she stood to her feet. For a second she had totally forgotten he was there.

'Did you?' she returned the question, before coughing slightly.

'Here, this envelope. But what have you found? What's that book you put back so quickly?

'Nothing, I was just wondering what it was myself. It doesn't look at all important to me; just a tatty old thing.' She had set herself a trap in not divulging the journal there and then. 'What's in that envelope?'

Carl drew several papers from the packet and laid them on the bed. Beverly took some of them and sifted through a few. Quickly discarding them, being afraid to bring them to his attention, though he had found some too, she thought it better to make light of them.

'I don't think any of these are death certificates. We should burn the lot,' she said, meaning to take a closer look at them on her own at a later time.

'You're right. No, hang on, I think it's here,' he opened out the large off white sheet, 'Yes, here it is.'

Beverly peered over his shoulder at the page as he read,

'Date and time of death; Monday July 5th, 1943. Emma Hopkins. Cause of death, tuberculosis. So she did die of tuberculosis. Well, what do we make of this bit of paper, Beverly?'

Beverly moved away from Carl and sat at the bottom end of the bed. Her cupped hands moved jerkily after she covered her face with them. Her sobs, quiet at first, troubled Carl. Remembering her sweet mother's embrace she allowed her grief to surface. It was the only embrace she remembered because of something special she had drawn at school when she was six, a mother's day card, with copious flowers and hearts. Her mother cherished it from the moment she received it. Everything her mother did was precious but that extra special memory would never be repeated. Carl, moved with compassion, sat beside her and hugged her tenderly. Tears ran down his face as pain seeped from his own wounds. This too would be a precious moment for both of them.

'I'll take you back home, Beverly.'

He gently eased her from the bed and together they took up their coats and left the house. Again in silence they drove the half hour journey back to Sittingbourne.

Thomas had finished in the garden in order to cook the midday meal. As they returned to the kitchen, he lifted the wooden spoon from the pan of brown rice he was cooking for dinner and invited Carl to stay. Feeling rather rejected and out of the picture, but feigning sympathy with the atmosphere, Thomas fell silent too and put the dinner on hold. Carl explained what had happened and after some recovery Thomas resumed cooking the mild lamb curry. Carl and Beverly ate what they could, after which Carl thanked and praised Thomas for the hot tasty dish. 'Would you like dessert? I've made a raspberry Pavlova.'

'I think we could both do with a dose of sugar. What do you think, Beverly?'

'Yes, please, I need something cool after that delicious curry,' she answered still shivering with emotional shock 'Thank you, Thomas.'

'It's very good of you to invite me,' Carl said, and then addressing Thomas asked,

'Do you have a mother?'

Thomas changed the subject, 'I hope you like the raspberries, they haven't quite thawed out yet but they're very tasty with a bit of a crunch.'

'Yes, they are pretty tasty but I meant, is your mother alive or has she died too?'

'The sweetness of the meringue is not too much? Actually I didn't make it, it's a shop bought one, you may have guessed.'

'I think it's a sore subject for Thomas,' Beverly interrupted.

Thomas quickly ate his own meringue while periodically and nervously squinting at Carl.

'Yes, I'd rather not talk about her if you don't mind.'

'Not at all, please accept my apologies for asking.' Carl focused on the rest of his dessert and when finished placed his spoon in the centre of his dish. 'I'll make a drink if you like.'

'No, I'll do that,' said Thomas, who was eager to escape from the awkward situation, 'but on second thoughts, I'll make it later, after I've washed up.' He needed to impress people. While trying to act humbly he cleared the dishes silently. Carl left for home when his offer of help with the dishes was declined. Beverly, whose offer was also declined, crept up the stairs to lie down, exhausted from the tears she had shed. She longed for Thomas to show some affection, to embrace her as her brother had. For two hours she yearned for a touch from him but there was only silence. As she lay there a blackbird's singing on a branch of the sycamore tree, which stood huge and proud a few feet from the narrow drive, sounded miles away. The country lane beyond concealed their home. She thought of Carl's embrace and the journal that had escaped his scrutiny. The cruelty of the moment, the regret of not divulging its contents brought more grief. Loneliness was not foreign to her. All those years of abuse, caught up in her mother's death certificate, finally taking their toll. She fell asleep.

An hour later she opened her eyes to look at the bedside clock, its luminous face read five o'clock exactly. Darkness had covered her with its nothingness. It was time to prepare tea for Thomas and her. Switching on the bedside light she swung her legs over the side of the bed to put on her clogs. Slowly she ventured down the oak staircase. Thomas, curled up in a ball, lay on the lounge settee, fast asleep. She stared at his fresh complexion, perusing his silent distance. Something must be bothering him too, she thought, and left the room. Chicken salad sandwiches were sure to please him. As she prepared one of his favourite dishes she heard him yawn loudly and anticipated his arrival in the kitchen.

'Beverly,' she turned at the sound of his croaky, just woken up voice. 'Let's go round to your dad's house. I need to settle some things in my own heart towards my own dad.'

'How will that help?'

'Just a thought, maybe the atmosphere of grief will help me get rid of some of mine.'

She cut the sandwiches slowly in half, 'I don't think it would. The house is awful. The sooner I get it sorted the better for all of us.' She handed him his portion and sat opposite so that any expression on his face would not be hidden from view.

'Well then, maybe if I helped instead of always running away from my own dad's death, it could work as a kind of surrogate.' He took his first bite.

'Perhaps, but I promised Paula… she will be coming at the weekend and we are planning that the two of us deal with the final two rooms.'

'I'm realizing that riches aren't everything. I cannot hide behind what we have here forever. I need to put my father to rest somehow. This seems an ideal opportunity.'

If she allowed him entry into the house he would have to be watched closely, 'It isn't your dad you will be putting to rest. It is your grief, Thomas.'

'Grief then, same thing.'

He ran his finger around the rim of the fruit bowl then picked up the same apple Beverly had earlier. They finished their meal without further conversation. Afterwards she slid from the stool and walked over to his side to remove his empty plate. He pushed her hand away and again reached for the apple. Crunching it using his left hand, he slid the other hand around her waist. At last, the touch she had been waiting for comforted her troubled soul; a little late and not as effective as it may have been but better than nothing.

'We'll ask Paula,' he stated, 'let's drive over to her straight after tea.'

'She's on duty till the weekend.'

'Ah, that's a pity.' He looked up at her while releasing his hold.

Beverly did not wish to reveal the secret to anybody but Paula. Even though she never kept a secret from Thomas, she had to keep this one. At least for now, just in case what bothered him was because of her.

'Tell you what,' suggested Beverly, 'as soon as Paula and I have finished sorting it out we can go round there, just the two of us and you can do and say all you have ever wanted to your own dad and see if it helps.'

'With the house empty? Of everything?'

'Yes, everything. Then we can close the door on both of our fathers in one day and live our lives somewhat healed.

Thomas gazed at the floor.

40

'Beverly.'

'Thomas?'

'I would like to go before Paula does, so let's go tonight, this evening, straight after this, while the grief is fresh from the events of today.'

Why the persistence? He had never been as pushy before and she too had noticed how he had not cleared himself entirely from earshot earlier. 'I, I'm actually feeling exhausted. I'd be happier to go tomorrow.'

'You are going to be running through the bedrooms right? Well, I'm sure Paula would be glad of the extra help. She may not need to come if we manage all the sorting.'

Normally a quiet man of thirty two, he became quite excited but tried to play it down. He was no actor, a good listener and could be assertive when things meant a lot to him. Beverly raised her head. The reflection of the white tiles above the sink she was now washing up at twinkled in her blue eyes. He stared, without standing, at her form but, as her back was turned, he could not detect the expression of horror on her face. She stood, unable to concentrate or plan her next move. How could she keep this up for much longer? She would have to tell him, but not just yet.

After preparing the kitchen for the following day's breakfast Beverly stated,

'I'm off to bed, got some reading to catch up on.' She kept out of the way of any further conversation until morning.

On waking early, she crept downstairs and brewed a cup of tea in the kitchen before carrying her filled mug to the lounge. She opened the lounge curtains and stood to watch the sun rise. It never took long as a row of pine trees hid most of the pink and orange hues. She sat in her favourite armchair opposite the ornate grandfather clock and, though the hands marched forward and the ticking continued, her memory of the first time she met Thomas wound its way back in time. It was July 21st, 1967, at a top consultant's retirement party at the hospital, at age twenty nine, that Thomas first laid eyes on her. Now in October, 1970, two years after their marriage, she wondered what he saw in her.

Why had he not chosen Paula and why marry a woman who always made wrong decisions and whose life was hampered by duty rather than being exuberant with joy and laughter. It stood to reason that she would serve him well and she did. He had insisted on a life without children and at that time she agreed. Thomas, the loner, yet the rich man, said he would give her a life of plenty. He had just achieved his medical consultancy and looked forward to an early retirement in this somewhat large and beautiful house. Her eyes fixed on the face of the grandfather clock. The mahogany enhanced its deep reddish brown against the pale pink wallpaper. The shadow of the clock suggested a continuous sunny day. The sun, always happy, always punctual, never without light even behind clouds during the day, blew her darkness into that shadow. It was her focal point, that shadow; her comforter because when she turned away from it, the sun, like a blackboard duster erasing mistakes made possibly a thousand times over, warmed her most tragic memories. Her mind flashed back to that first time. Then to how accurate and attentive he was towards his patients; a real blue eyed boy with a smile that only appeared when she had passed by him on his ward round and it was the other nurses observations that brought it to her attention. They told her he was usually a lonely, dull physician. She fathomed even then that he must be disadvantaged with some problem breaking his heart. Knowing his smile appeared only for her, she knew she could be a solution to his heartache. He was not an attractive man but that smile lit up his face, just like on extremely rare occasions a smile lit up her father's face and it was not dissimilar to his at such times. Living with her it would remain for as long as she was with him. How wrong she was! He only smiled and became excited when getting his way. He always had his way, but times such as these, when Carl insisted that he talk to Beverly privately, that smile disappeared. Now, it reappeared at the prospect of going to her dad's house to deal with his grief.

She snapped out of her dream state as Thomas suddenly emerged for his breakfast. The shock almost choked her.

'Good morning,' he greeted her chirpily.

'Hi,' she managed.

'So, what time do we set off?'

'After breakfast and the tidying is done.'

'Okay, boss.'

Who was boss? It surely wasn't her, but she kept silent. It was always better to give way at times like this, to keep his smile going.

Beverly cooked a full English breakfast for Thomas but had no appetite for one herself. A slice of toast and marmalade would suffice until she was in a happier mood. As Thomas enjoyed mouthful after mouthful without looking up Beverly carried her empty plate to the sink behind her. After laying it on the draining board to wait for his, she crossed the kitchen to fill the kettle once more.

'Would you like toast with your tea, Thomas?'

'I always have toast with my tea, of course.'

Of course, she thought, *silly me*.

'While you are eating that I will tidy around and then we can go.'

She finished the tidying and the last bits of the washing up then gave a shout to Thomas who had disappeared upstairs to clean his teeth.

She observed broad sunbeams piercing the drive through the pine trees when she opened the door to leave. Thomas took up the car keys from the small oak table in the hall and followed, without a word, Beverly to the car. She had plenty of time to think on their journey, as she pretended to sleep. Planning the grief release routine was imperative. She would keep him in the finished parts of the house for as long as possible explaining that her father's and brothers' unwanted possessions, if they were still present, would distract him from thinking of his own father.

She wished she had removed the journal from its place and given it to Paula to keep instead of the stress she had in keeping it in the library. Why did she so easily give way? It was a weakness caused by the violence of her father, she knew that, anything to stay out of harm's way, please him; please Thomas; please everybody. That's it! She would hide the journal in Paula's bag for now. It's the only place it would be safe and then she would have to trust Paula to keep it under lock and key. She would have to bring it with her when they meet in future and would have to swear not to read it. It was their policy never to go into other people's property but this would have to be an exception. She came to when the wheels ran over the gravel driveway. Once out of the car Beverly walked before Thomas to unlock the front door. He followed her into the house eagerly yet in trepidation. After listening to her recommendations, he insisted on the entire house being used. The beige walls and dirty carpets made him cringe. He had never been here before and never wanted to after Beverly's many descriptions of the place. This would be his one and only mission. As long as Beverly was the help he needed everything was fine and she would be of great use to him in the future. He knew of the abuse that went on in the house but not in any great detail. He didn't seem to want to know either. He understood the way grief works. It weakens a person greatly and she, weak now, was not in a position to argue too much. Thomas's father died around the same time as Beverly's, but he wanted nothing to do with his funeral, he had said. That little piece of paper Carl revealed changed his mind.

Beverly led him to the lounge where he genuinely began to pay his disrespects to his father. The empty room exposed the hollow state of his heart which filled with a sudden anger. His father had not given him all he wanted and asked for. The affections of his father were not at all satisfactory towards him. He never embraced him. Oh yes, he made sure he had plenty and more than most children but not what he really wanted; a love; a closeness of father and son. The looks he got whenever he did see him were icy cold, even inhuman at times. How could he enjoy all that his dad provided without a glimmer of a bond between them? And how could they bond? He was never there. His father had left his mother when Thomas was just a baby. He would only be seen for a brief second when Thomas visited his mother after long intervals, mostly during boarding school holidays. They were enough, those frozen encounters.

'I will never be able to bond with my own father!' he shouted towards Beverly.

The loosening of pain disturbed her. She had never seen him like this. His silent distance is what was familiar to her. Redirecting his attention she pointed out, 'You must direct your words to him, Thomas, not to me or I will have to leave the room.'

His cool response came immediately, 'You were right, something in the room would distract me so you can leave and come back when I'm finished.'

At this she took the opportunity to get to her father's bedroom quickly. Pulling the journal from its place she realized she had left

Paula's bag in the lounge. She thought she may manage to reach a hand in without him noticing so retraced her steps, only to find the door closed. All was silent but she knocked quickly and entered.

'I forgot my bag,' she said and, in a hurry, grabbed it and left.

Thomas did not comment even though he knew it wasn't hers. He was too preoccupied with the silent shock at his own anger to notice her entrance. Upstairs, Beverly picked up the journal and, praying that Paula would forgive her, she opened the bag and, careful not to disturb what was inside, quickly slid it in. The bag was big enough to hold it comfortably without shifting anything much and because of the policy they had of not going into one another's things, she was afraid to have it on her conscience to look inside but for a brief moment. She closed the bag and returned downstairs to see how Thomas was getting on. After knocking, she waited for his invitation to rejoin him. A quarter of a minute passed before he answered, 'Come in.'

Opening the door slightly and peeping around it she asked, 'Are you finished?'

'I think I've said all I'm going to.'

She opened the door wider after quickly replacing Paula's bag then stood watching and waiting for any further invitation. Thomas, kneeling on the floor with his head in his hands, did not look up. She stifled a sigh of relief that he had not observed the return of the bag. She could at least forget about the journal now and stepped over to enfold Thomas in her arms. At her touch he began to sob uncontrollably. A full quarter of an hour later he sat up straight, exhausted from the outburst. Beverly let go and smoothed his forehead where it had developed the deep lines of a frown.

'Do you want to go through the other rooms now?' she asked.

'I think I will and get it all out.'

'Then I will stay with you until it is over.'

He smiled as she led him hand in hand to the other rooms downstairs. He tried to drum up any lurking grief and anger but he was emotionally spent.

Beverly led him up the stairs to her dad's bedroom. He hated the place. It spoke of too much poverty, too much clutter. He began, after the slight interlude and to impress Beverly,

'This is how much you made me feel on the inside; many cluttering thoughts. Too much material stuff you never said no to. That stuff which could never take your place.' He imagined his father actually being in the room. 'I never once visited your home, never sat on your knee. I had to live a life in boarding school, away even from my mother, an orphan practically. At her house there was everything material waiting for me, except she wouldn't let me into her most precious rooms,' he started to shout, 'and I am not your son, never was and never will be. Twice dead!! You and me.'

'And me,' comforted Beverly.

He turned towards her and searching her for answers, yet finding none, he continued quite unexpectedly, 'Shall we sort stuff out? I've said it all, what else is there?'

She reminded him, 'I promised Paula. She will be coming at the weekend.'

'Why not take her out instead for a meal or something? We can do quite a bit today by ourselves.'

'Well, I'd rather not; she and I need time together.'

'Why, we do too, we can at least do half an hour to make the burden lighter. I will at least tidy the locker and you can help if you want but maybe you could make a cup of tea?'

Beverly agreed to the tea and left the room. He wasted no time in turning to the locker. He had taken note when Carl told him what he had found in the drawer and that there had been papers in the cupboard. He opened the door to the cupboard but it was empty. He assumed what had been in the cupboard were the papers stacked in two ragged piles on the bed. It would only take Beverly five minutes, more or less, to make the tea. 'Beverly!' he shouted.

'Yes.'

'I'm feeling pretty low on blood sugar. Any chance you could nip round to the shop for some biscuits, cake or something?'

'Yes, I'm hungry too; I'll go and get some.'

46

He heard the door slam and having bought more time he sat on the bed, picked up one untidy pile and started to leaf through. He had at least fifteen minutes so thumbed through it, not too fast, and read every one of the mostly love letters between Ralph and Emma. They were dated way back before their marriage and not of great significance to him. Whenever he read the word, 'love' he skipped over it as a piercing pain would enter his heart. Because of the rules that only he was aware of, concerning love, and the presence of unhealed wounds, he could never truly love Beverly like that, never say, 'love', and mean it, never touch her with any sense of togetherness, not like Ralph and Emma. Just shows how love is not worth the hassle as parting is the only reaping of such bonding. He would never bond again, with anyone. He would only love himself, to avoid getting hurt. Let them love him, give all they are willing to, but he would never respond, never open up to let them in or they will never leave, not even at death. He knew only too well since the grieving downstairs that his dad remains, why else would he be searching? Beverly had said she wanted them to leave the house, close the door and be healed all in one day. Comforting words, but how true would or could they possibly be? When he had picked up the fifth letter he had found a small white envelope which could easily have been missed if he had been leafing through at a faster pace. He had put it aside to read last and had already read the message on the front, 'To whoever finds me first:'

When he finished the other pointless letters, he glanced at his watch. He had enough time to open it before Beverly returned. Tearing the sealed right hand corner he slid his thumb across the top apprehensively revealing the folded paper inside. He unfolded it. The writing was not too long. It read: 'If you are reading this after unsealing the envelope, this is for you. I am a dying man and should I die before I can say anything to any of my existing family, then I simply ask that you tell my children that I loved them, that I always loved them. There is a journal, one I wrote since my wife died. You will find it just opposite on the shelf, next to the Bible. Tell my children I loved them and love them still. This journal will explain it all, will tell of my life, will tell...' Thomas looked up before adding, 'Of me.' That was it, no more was written but he had signed it, Ralph.

Swiftly, Thomas turned towards the library. He heard the front door slam again. Beverly was back. He fumbled quickly, scanning the spines but could not find any journal; the Bible, yes, but no journal. His scrutiny of the shelves left him frustrated. He should have been able to find it without any trouble as he was the first to read the letter. Then he noticed a dint in the dust. A sure sign it had been removed recently. Who could have removed it? It could only have been Carl. He was the one who had found the small piece of paper. Even if he, wait a minute, he said that Beverly had been looking through the library but had found nothing. So it couldn't have been there then. The only other person, to his knowledge who had been helping, was Paula.

'Tea, Thomas!'

'Tea? Um, okay, just coming.' He quickly refolded the letter and put it back into the envelope leaving everything else on the bed exactly where he found it. Nobody would know it was he who had read it unless forensics examined it and that was hardly likely. How could he tell Ralph's children that he loved them? Giving them the message would remove all significance from his own life and he counted, a lot. He would say nothing, not even for a dead man's wishes, to anybody. He would find that journal to see what was written in its pages but first he had to find out for sure who had taken it and how many knew about its existence. He would not be able to ask any of the children directly so to bide his time he took to the stairs for that much needed cup of tea.

'How's it going?' shouted Beverly from the kitchen.

'Just fine, absolutely fine,' he shouted back, grinning as he descended the last step. He strode along the hall to pick up his chipped mug of tea then sat on the worn out three legged stool. Beverly handed him the opened packet of biscuits she had bought. He whisked two away quickly. His thoughts remained with the missing journal which furrowed his brow a little harsher than she had seen in the lounge.

'Are you okay? What did you manage to do upstairs?'

'Nothing, I felt too weak, just rummaged through my thoughts and emotions to get any extra healing. It'll be great to finally shut the door on grief. I must say this is a great way of dealing with it. It's great to have you around for this, Beverly. I'm back to work tomorrow so will have to be in peak form for that.'

'Very true; so Paula and I will finish at the weekend, or it may take two weekends or even more, who knows, depends on our shifts. I don't think I can face too much more today. I'd love to go home and rest for a bit.'

Thomas stared into his mug which held the final mouthful. Shallow. He would have to act shallowly. Thinking of how he obtains information from his patients, in order to diagnose their illnesses, he knew this was a far more complicated issue and so required sensitive specialist handling. To extract a family journal from someone else, more than likely Paula and, if not, another member of the family, he would have to be discreet, act like he knows nothing, yet questioning silently every move anyone makes from now on. When the time is right he would either let them know he knows about the journal or simply, by observation alone, discover and confiscate it. Either way he knew he was in for a long wait.

Chapter Three

The following night, Friday, Beverly thought long and hard while Thomas was working out in their gym in the basement, about what to do with the journal in Paula's bag. As she sat in the lounge staring at the grandfather clock the tall brass lamp beside it refused to cast her focal point. Ideas never came easy for her and especially without her shadow. Carl, having said he would take more responsibility, remained a problem so she could not risk returning it to the library. If she brought it home Thomas would find it. She hated stress and would much rather everything be brought out into the open. No, she and Paula had to read it together as planned. Even what they found out about the extra brother and 'her' could not possibly be forwarded until they located them, if they still existed. She left for an early night knowing something would come to mind, it had to.

When Thomas finally joined her in the lounge, he, exhausted from exercising his body and her from exercising her mind, they decided on an early-ish night. After showering and donning their night attire both lay side by side in bed, each in separate worlds. Turning on their sides and facing away from each other they closed their eyes, Thomas, thinking about getting to Paula and the journal. Beverly; thinking about Thomas, Paula, Carl, the journal and the death bed of her father, besides a myriad of other things. Both slept soundly once sleep came and on arising early the following morning, before Thomas woke up, Beverly lifted her turquoise silk dressing gown from the back of the bedroom door and slipped it on. Creeping downstairs in her feather light slippers she made her way to the kitchen before brewing a most welcome cup of tea and carried it steadily to the lounge. She sat and sipped the hot beverage from her favourite bone china mug. She missed her faithful shadow and with three hours to go before she would be meeting Paula at nine o'clock she would have to imagine it. The Master of the House, as she had nicknamed the clock, struck six. Thomas would not hear it as his deep sleep snuffed out the sound, plus the bedroom was far enough away for him not to be disturbed by its chiming. She left the door open in order to hear him coming down the stairs and sat silently until, at last, the idea leapt from the bottom of her mug as she downed the last mouthful. She would arrive at the house half an hour earlier, remove the journal then place it back in the library. Carl would not be coming around. It had been agreed that he allow Beverly and Paula to get on with what they had started together.

Thomas entered the lounge just as quietly as she had descended the stairs, fully dressed and ready for work. 'Good morning,' he boomed across the airwaves.

She jumped up before replying with a soft, 'Good morning. I'm just about to cook breakfast. Are you going for your usual walk in the garden?' Without waiting for his answer she picked up her mug and walked sleepily back to the kitchen. The sudden change in him could have fooled her into believing his healing was complete and his attitude towards her, changed forever. Any release of pain, in her experience, was sure to bring about a temporary fresh surge of energy once a person had settled down then the cycle would begin all over again.

Following her to the kitchen he set the breakfast counter which was normally her job in the mornings. The atmosphere clamoured for her discernment. Why couldn't he just be his normal distant self than putting on a display of spoilt rottenness? Nevertheless, she went along with the change and handed him his never changing breakfast dish.

'So you are off to your dad's. If you find anything let me know. I would love to know what the note Carl found meant.'

'No problem,' Beverly had no intention to let him know anything. She would not allow too many hands or heads to work on this until it was solved by herself and Paula.

Thomas smiled weakly at the flat answer. 'Will nothing cheer you up today?' he asked.

'Not much, too much going on. You better brush your jacket, it's got a bit of fluff on the collar.

He brushed it off without looking, slid off his stool and made his way, slightly rebuffed by her lack of response to his exuberance, to the front door. 'See you later,' he shouted.

Beverly remained silent.

After Thomas left for work she dressed in her everyday working clothes and within the hour she had reached her father's house. She turned off the ignition and made her way briskly down the garden path. Heavy clouds darkened the house so she switched on the lights. Paula's bag was her target. She picked it up, reached in without looking, and pulled out the journal then glanced down and was about to close the bag when she noticed a page hanging from the journal. She took a closer look in case it had fallen from within the journal but it couldn't have as it would have crumpled when she pushed it into the bag. She removed it from the journal before laying the journal on the floor. The page that she had taken pains to instruct her sister not to read until they reached it together revealed a tragic betrayal of trust. Her mind swirled, the room span around and around as though she was about to faint. She leaned on the wall for balance. *She can't have, Paula can't have ripped out that page.* She would have to confront her now but how? She stared for a while at both objects wondering what to do and finally decided to save the stress. She would replace the journal and say nothing. At least she knew where it was and could not be lied to any further when they came to the end of book and she already knew what was written in it. It was not worth losing Paula over. From now on she would not let Paula out of her sight. What if the entire journal disappeared?

Paula's knock made Beverly return the page to her bag at top speed. She opened the door to her estranged sister. Paula was the first to give a greeting, 'Hello Beverly.'

'Hi, come in. How's your week been?' she asked flatly.

'Very busy, how about yours?' Paula replied while stepping into the hall and hanging up her coat.

'It would take forever to tell you. Before we start sorting lets have a cup of tea. I need to talk to you.' The firmness Paula had not heard in her sister's tone told her the issue was serious but she dare not cast her mind too far back. Any sign of trouble and she would flee from the house.

'Oh, I forgot my bag when I left last week. Here it is.' She lifted it and guarded it like its life depended on her.

'Sit down, Paula; I'll bring in the tea when it's done.'

Paula sat alone in the lounge clutching her bag on the edge of a chair opposite the front window. The furniture was all that was left from the sort out. Her cheeks grew slightly flushed but she waited, hoping it was not about what was in her bag. Beverly did not want to deal with the matter either. Besides Paula wasn't the type of person to have done what she did so she would try to calm down and treat her gently while coming straight to the point. She left the kitchen with the scalding tea and handed one of the two chipped mugs to Paula. Putting her own mug on the small table in front of her Beverly looked directly at Paula, studying her innocence. No, she had not been innocent but that did not make her a guilty character. She was, in fact, a very simple and matter of fact person, never usually stepping out of line. 'I can't understand, Paula, what made you tear the page out of the journal. What made you do that, even after we made an agreement to get to that page when we came to it? I wasn't trying to hide it from you. Have you read it?'

'Have you been looking in my bag?' asked Paula defensively.

'No, I haven't, but I had to open it to hide the journal from Carl. I came in early today to put it back on the shelf. Carl came in to help the other day then Thomas the day after. He wanted to deal with the grief of losing his dad and to help out a bit. I opened your bag, without looking inside, and put the journal in. It was the only safe place I could think of. When I took it out this morning that page was hanging on under my fingers by a corner, because I didn't look what I was doing. If I had been looking I would have left the page where it was and may not have discovered it was that last page.'

Paula lifted her mug to her quivering lips then put it down again. 'I took it out because you are always in charge. I am the underdog, always taking orders from you, and Carl. I thought that for once in my life I could take charge, just once and that was the only way I could. Take it behind your back. Now, I've said it.'

'Paula, don't you realize that this is a very serious state of affairs we are going through? That is so unreasonable and taking such a step to totally destroy our trust or rather my trust in you. I have no words to describe how that feels. I almost passed out when I saw it in your bag.'

'Beverly, even when I was taking it I went almost purple with guilt and felt so awful that I was going to come in today and put it straight back. You wouldn't have even found out if it wasn't for those two men coming in.'

'Maybe not, but I have found out. Either I can trust you or not. We need to read that together and get to that page together. Have you read it, Paula?' repeated Beverly.

'No, how could I? I forgot to take my bag with me when we left each other last week. When I was here with you that day, you would have caught me reading it so I just shoved it in my bag, carefully.'

Beverly stood up, then sat down, then squinted at her tea and finally took the mug in both hands as if to warm them and said, 'I have enough stress with what Carl found in the drawer upstairs and with Thomas's funny kind of behaviour recently. I know Thomas has always been a bit preoccupied with himself but he worries me. Please, let's trust each other. Will you allow me that much? I need you to be my friend.'

'Okay, I apologize, it was such a horrid feeling anyway and I never want to feel it again. We can deal with this together. I will keep straight from now on, I promise. What did Carl find?'

Beverly explained the entire week's events.

'What about Sidney? Where is he? Has he not been in touch at all?' Paula asked while twiddling her hair.

'No, I haven't heard anything. He's not the type to get involved anyway, poor thing. We'll take him as we find him if he ever does show up.'

'Yes, he's bound to at some point, surely. Shall I wash the mugs or leave them for our next cup of tea?' asked Paula.

'Leave them, let's get started. We can read the next bit of the journal first if you like. What do you think? You see I'm already giving you some responsibility.'

Paula chuckled. She looked up to her sister and had done throughout her childhood but could not quite understand her. At times tension between them had been severe and especially when Beverly was stressed and at such times Paula only thought of herself, after all she was only a child and had not developed the art of reasoning things out. In her view Beverly always seemed to know exactly what to do and never showed any emotion. How could she know the pressure of being immediately under those in authority, especially cruel authority? She didn't understand just how hard it was for Beverly to make decisions nor how she felt about herself. Beverly, a soldier under orders, had to give orders. It was as simple as that. There was no time to just be sisters and enjoy one another, but that was about to change.

Once again they mounted the threadbare stairs to their father's bedroom. Beverly carried the journal. As she entered the room she stopped for a second before saying, 'Oh, I forgot about those.'

'What?'

'Those papers on the bed, I told Carl it would be better to burn them but I didn't mean it, just wanted to put him off looking at them. We'll sort them out first.' She took one pile, handed it to Paula then took the other for herself. 'On second thoughts let's read these together as well and if we find anything of importance we can keep them, if not, we can ditch them or maybe keep them as family history. That's a thought; we can start a history project for future generations.'

As they went through the letters, taking their alternative turns, both sisters felt they were intruding on very private lives. They read about their parents' memories of times at home and their intense relationship with each other but nothing out of the ordinary that could influence any other life. Paula finally came across the white envelope that Thomas had left. 'Here's an envelope and it says "To whoever reads me first." Shall I take what's in there out, Beverly?'

'Yes, of course, we will read everything, not a page unturned.'

Paula drew out the folded paper, opened it and started to read what it said out loud. '"If you are reading this after unsealing the envelope, this is for you. I am a dying man and should I die before I can say anything to any of my existing family then I simply ask that you tell my children that I loved them."'

'Wait a minute,' said Beverly, 'those are dad's words. Remember I told you. Let me see that. That first sentence says, "Unsealing it", did you unseal that? You didn't did you, did you?'

'No, it was already opened.'

'Read the rest.'

'"that I always loved them. There is a journal, one I wrote since my wife died. You will find it just opposite on the shelf, next to the Bible. Tell my children I loved them and love them still. This journal will explain it all, will tell of my life, will tell…'

Beverly sat wide eyed and shocked to the core. 'Somebody somewhere knows about the journal. Carl would surely have told me. I'm all goose pimples.'

'Could it have been Thomas?' asked Paula, twiddling her hair again.

'If he knows about it he hasn't told me and I haven't told him. We simply cannot admit to having it, not until we find out what has happened to that son and 'her'. We have to find them but, Paula, I know what is on that last page but we must find out everything first. We will have to get through it quicker now because whoever knows about it could well be looking for it. Promise me that if anybody asks you, you will never tell them and even if Thomas should ask you where it is, say nothing. Don't assume I have told him anything. Until I find out what is bugging him I can't entirely trust him.'

They read the rest of the letters that only told of the dating between Ralph and Emma and of one another missing each other so much. 'He must have cried a lot seeing those tissues everywhere,' observed Beverly. 'There was no mention or even a hint of anyone else, except on that one small piece of paper that Carl had found. There's not much about what he was actually doing in the Navy in those letters either; just reassurances of the wedding plans, dates and how each other was. Let's carry on reading the next entry. If mum ever found out about 'her' and her son she would have been devastated.'

Beverly picked up the journal but before she started to read Paula reached into her bag and pulled out the missing page. Beverly was concerned about it being loose and the page that corresponded with it. If only Paula hadn't of done that, the journal could be a priceless piece of writing. Only time would tell of its contents.

'We are going to have to put this somewhere where nobody will find it. I can't keep it because of Thomas and, well, are you sure I can trust you now, Paula? Look me in the eye and promise you will keep this safe. There is nobody else. Promise me again. It will have to be a contract between us. Look, I'll write out a receipt that you have it and where exactly you will be keeping it but in code. We will call it your

Christmas card list, nobody would be interested in that. Just in case somebody gets hold of this record and reads it. I can't take any chances. Tell you what, I won't take it out of my purse; that way I'll have it at all times.' Beverly wrote the contract and Paula signed it entrusting Beverly to remind her, and vice versa, of its whereabouts if they ever forgot or lost their records or the unforeseen ever happened. Beverly tapped the pen on the paper a few times as if to seal the agreement. 'I must remember this is where the journal is and not your Christmas card list.' she laughed. She replaced the page Paula handed her and pressed it closed as if to cement it in then opened the journal at the page they left off last time. 'Are you ready?'

'Yes.'

'We read about him being all at sea and without hope and found out about 'her' and the son. I'll carry on, "How do I look after my sons and daughters? They are so small; too young to have lost their mother. Carl is only eight and full of life. His dark wavy hair reminds me of Emma so much. He has her nose too. He wants so much to please me and readily does all I ask, possibly due to the way I ask him. I have to remind myself that he is only eight and not expect too much perfection. Then there's Beverly with her fair hair and blue, crystal clear eyes, so full of love and warmth. She is more like me when I was young, to look at; rosy cheeks when she is tired and dimples when she laughs, six years old. Only two months have passed since Emma's passing but Beverly is as keen as Carl to help in her own little way. She's such a sweetheart. Sidney next and quite a handful I must say, getting into all kinds of mischief at four years old. If I try to get Carl and his sisters to talk to him or vice versa, he's off round the room like a firecracker. Never still. What a little tearaway but he seems somewhat aloof from his brothers and sisters. He also is more like me in looks but in mannerisms, rather like Emma; just the way he lifts his arms when he wants to carry things or wants me to carry him. How can I resist? I can't explain why that reminds me of Emma, it just does. Last of all there is Paula. She is quite a shy little girl of two. What a bright little thing she is and white hair to match. Her grey eyes are the colour of Emma's. I can't help wanting to cry when I look into her eyes. If it wasn't for her round baby face I could swear it was Emma. I have to keep my eye on her though and forget that she reminds me too much of Emma or my grief would forever haunt me and I would be useless to her. I am forever asking the others to help her out when she is eating, going to the toilet etc. She is a little darling. I would never part from my children. And I certainly will not let, 'her' look after them. She will never enter my house and neither will her boy, even if he is my son. But with 'her' constant threats to my sanity and persistent demands on my fatherhood to the son she wanted, not me, could prove more of a struggle than I want it to be; having said that I acknowledge my responsibility towards Thomas. He is my son even if I hate 'her' but try as I might I cannot bring myself to love him. I never voluntarily brought him into the world. But, she asks far too much from me. '" Beverly placed a marker in the journal and closed it. 'That's that entry, Paula. We should do some sorting now. Wouldn't it be great to find some photographs of when we were small? To read a description is good enough but not the best.'

'He said his son is called Thomas,' pointed out Paula.

'Where?'

'You just read it.' Paula pointed to it.

'It must be a coincidence; there's plenty of Thomases around and at least we know his first name was Thomas, we just need her name and surname and we have him.'

'It would be quite something if your husband was him, wouldn't it?'

'Yes, it would, but it can't be him. How on earth would he know us, what we look like and all that? It certainly would be an incredible coincidence. Besides, finding that out would be an enormous task and far too much stress. I imagine her son to be far more pompous than my Thomas with a mother like that.'

'He'd be your half sister too, so maybe not. People don't marry their sisters.'

Beverly laughed and corrected Paula, 'No, and I never thought of that. I couldn't even imagine being married to a half brother, not a half sister! We need extra boxes so let's go round the shop to get some.'

'Okay, maybe we can get some chocolate as well.'

As they walked into the shop Mr Farlow had already anticipated they would need more and had a pile ready and waiting.

'Thanks for looking out for us,' said Beverly as they carried them out.

'Any time and, Paula, it's good to see you again but maybe if there is a next time it will be during happier times for you all.'

'I hope so too, thanks again, bye for now.'

On there return they sorted out half of the boys bedroom.

'Imagine, nothing touched for almost twenty years in here. I will give dad the compliment in keeping his home clean – ship shape. Once we were gone he had to do it all by himself. Fancy, he threw us out but kept our stuff,' Beverly giggled.

Paula, now aged thirty one, stood vulnerably before Beverly. Her memory wound back sixteen years. Time had stood still regarding the pain of those years. She had tried to put it behind her many times but there was always something, somewhere to trigger it off again and now facing it again she may not have this opportunity to pour out her heart to her sister. To let go of the aloneness of those years she began, 'Beverly, can we sit down for a bit? I need to say something.' They sat on the edge of Paula's old bed. Beverly waited in silence, 'Fifteen years ago, almost to the day, I was still here, on my own with him. Trying to do homework from school without any help from him and working in the house. Once you were gone it was very hard work. I did miss you but had to learn how to organize it all as you were the one, as I said, who gave all the orders. It did me good though and made me more independent. But I learned a bit about dad. He hardly ever spoke to me; just made sure I knew what I was doing. I actually had to take all the work on board that all three of you once did. There was me and Sidney for a year but Sidney was always messing about. He would look out of windows, getting distracted by dogs barking. The minute he heard one he dropped everything and charged, well, you know that and it didn't stop when you left. It was frustrating to say the least and in a way I was glad when dad found him a job on that farm. He so doted on animals. And it meant dad would stop punishing him for being so absent minded all the time. Dad could not tolerate him and his high energy and flightiness. He so disciplined poor Sidney that I would find Sidney totally beside himself with worry and he was terrified and more so when Carl and you left. He was the brunt then and copped everything. I really don't think dad cared that Sidney was a human being. It was as if he was in a trance when belting him. Like, in some other world. How many men treat their own sons that way? It's no wonder Sidney is so quiet, even with us the other day he didn't say a word, just complied with all that was said. I don't think he has ever grown up since mum died, not really.'

The two of them stared at each other for a few seconds.

'Carry on, Paula, this is as important as the journal. I want to know more about dad and how he was with you and Sidney.'

'How can it be true that dad loved us, Beverly? How?'

'Well, you saw in the journal when we were small how he loved us. He adored us all.'

'Yes, but how does a person change from being such a saint into acting like the demon he was?'

'I'm sure we will find out as we read but tell me a bit more about him after I left and then after Sidney left.'

'After you left and there was just Sidney and me dad kind of died a bit, I think. It's the only way I can describe it. When Carl left, he didn't seem to care that much. Well, he never cared but you know. Then when you left, he became even more bad tempered. Sidney was such a sore torment to him. Dad shouted and screamed at him constantly. I saw the veins bulging on his neck, dad's neck and I was convinced he'd have a heart attack. One day he came home from work, Sidney was standing stock still and as pale as anything I have ever seen. Dad called his name but he didn't answer, then he peered right into his eyes from about an inch away. Sidney didn't respond. He was in lockdown, Beverly. I wanted to get on with my work but I just had to watch what dad would do. We were all in the hall so dad hadn't gone very far when faced with this. He never once said anything to me. Like, he was seething and fuming because he couldn't get passed Sidney. As he stared at Sidney and continued to hurl rage in his face, shouting and eventually shouting that he was a good for nothing young brat, a silent tear leapt from Sidney's left eye and then another and another but he didn't move. The years he had suffered from dad, the scapegoat, he stood like Lot's wife, a pillar of salt. I didn't quite know what to do but I did pray, "Help him, God."' A solitary tear fell from Paula's eyes. She tasted the salty water as it scurried down her cheeks and into her slightly open mouth, in sympathy of that little fifteen year old boy. Beverly moved closer to her and laid a hand on her shoulder. 'Dad, started to punch him and punch him so hard but he still stood like a rock!'

Beverly squirmed at the tragic news. Sidney, so distant; not like Thomas; at least Thomas spoke to people and showed some humanity. She wondered what excuse Thomas had but Sidney's concrete exterior was far more perplexing than anything Thomas had shown. She started to think about Sidney in a new light. 'It's trauma, Paula. We are nurses, not mental nurses but still we can understand a little of what happens to a person who is constantly going through trauma. They do shut down after a while, can't take it.'

'No.'

'So how did Sidney get out of it?'

'I kept praying that God would help him. Finally, after dad could punch him no more, dad crumpled to the ground. He could not budge Sidney, no matter what and it burned him out. He lay like a five year old completely exhausted and started to sob. I crept over to Sidney and started to stroke him. I stroked his hair, his face and his hands and tried to reassure him. It was about, I don't know, about twenty minutes, it looked like dad had fallen asleep on the floor. Sidney's stone like face eventually gave way to a slight tremor. He started to shiver and breathe harder. I called him and he gradually turned to me. His eyes glazed and he started to open his mouth but it wouldn't open. I told him to stay there and went to make a cup of tea. When I came back I gave him the cup and tried to make him hold it but he couldn't so I lifted it to his lips and let him feel the heat. He took a small sip and it took me a good five minutes to get him to drink just half a cup. He didn't drink more after that but managed to move his head to look down at his father, "Why does dad hate me so much?" he whispered. All I could do was look at dad too. Eventually we crouched to examine him then stood up and, leaving him alone went into the kitchen to make some scrambled egg. Sidney was okay - ish afterwards but he has never recovered, has he?'

Beverly silently picked up a book from the small bedside table and laying it in a box, replied, 'No, he probably never will now, not at this stage in his life but, you never know, he might. Do you want some tea now, Paula?'

'I'll just tell you what happened when dad woke up. Actually, we never knew much about drink and drunkenness but I'm pretty sure he might have been drunk when he came in. Anyway, he finally came to and demanded something to eat so we made him scrambled eggs too.

There wasn't much else really. After he staggered to his feet and had eaten he started to shake. Sidney left the room. Dad followed him. I followed them both. I was convinced Sidney was in for some more of a beating and he must have done as well. He walked calmly into his bedroom and stood in a corner, facing dad's approach. Dad stood looking at him for a bit and then pled, "Sidney, please forgive me. Please forgive me, please forgive me." Then he sobbed. Sidney reached out to his dad but not too far. Dad took hold of Sidney's hands and held them for a bit and then the next thing I knew they were really hugging each other. Beverly, I think the real reasons for dad's behaviour must be written in the journal. It was too late though, so much damage had been caused to Sidney. He was never the same again but dad started to love him.'

'Wow, he did?'

'Yes, but once Sidney was sixteen it was out with him. Dad cared enough to find him the farm job and asked the farmer if Sidney could live at the farm. He knew Sidney was fragile by then; that he suffered greatly on the inside. He knew animals and being at a relative distance from humans would be good for him. Dad visited him as much as he could after that.'

Beverly emptied out one of the drawers in the chest of drawers. Removing an old jumper she wondered how she ever fitted into it. The brilliant yellow had turned into a dirty cream colour. The musty smell as she opened it out caused her to step back.

'I can't actually remember wearing this at all,' she stated, as Paula stood watching.

'Yes, carry on, Paula; I am listening at the same time as carrying on with this. 'So, once Sidney had left you were alone with dad. Actually, are you ready for some tea yet? You can tell me about your time with dad once we've had a drink. I'll open a window to give the room as chance to air.'

Paula remained quiet for a few seconds then bending down to pick up a sock that had fallen on the floor she surprised Beverly, saying, 'I would love to go home after a drink. Would you like to come to my place? We can cook something and talk some more after we've relaxed a bit.'

Beverly ran her hand down the back of her hair before answering, 'I'll have to ask Thomas so we can drop by on the way to your house. We can say you don't feel well or something and he might be okay with that. Actually, I have had an idea. I really would love to get through the journal a bit quicker. Let's finish sorting the house and then you can pretend you get ill. I can tell Thomas that I will have to come and stay to look after you. He won't mind that but if I just wanted to come and stay with you for no reason he wouldn't like it but whatever; he can look after himself for a few days. What do you think? He should be home by now.'

'Don't say I'm ill today, just that you want to come this afternoon to keep me company or something or that I simply invited you, which is true.'

'He may not like that but we can try.'

Beverly led the way out to her car and set off. Paula followed in her own car.

On arrival Beverly switched off the engine removed the keys and fumbled slightly nervously for the front door key. Putting the key in the brass key hole she turned it. Paula waited to the side of her. Both felt pangs of fear but were confident that the plan would work. Walking through the hall and kitchen and then on out of the back door they found Thomas in the garden pruning shrubs. Gardening was his favourite past time and the place of his focal point. The pink and white flowers of the Japanese anemone took centre stage. Paula remained quiet, stopping to admire the beauty of such a prestigious wonderland. Compared to her two bedroom flat this was a palace. Thomas and Beverly surely were blessed. Paula had become afraid of men because of all the abuse she had suffered and especially so during the final year of living with her father. She knew that much kindness, as she experienced when very young, could turn into savagery later on. The soft and luscious green of the grass beneath her feet seemed to spring up to greet her. She bathed in its glory while Beverly's request made its way into Thomas's ear. He had been deep in thought, thinking of his future, mulling over various things and hated being disturbed at such times. Beverly's gentle approach and smooth words allayed any adverse reaction from him.

'You want to stay at Paula's for the rest of the day?' he turned to see what invaded his peripheral vision; Paula fiddling with her scarf; the scarf Sidney bought her with his first set of wages. She loved its greens and oranges almost overlapping each other, the twists and turns of the pattern kept her mesmerized, especially when nervous. Irish colours reminded her of her Irish roots. Her geography teacher had asked one time if anyone had Irish roots. She had no idea. The first thing she asked her father that evening, after cooking his supper and cleaning his shoes in readiness for the following day's work, was if he knew of any Irish in the family. His unexpected answer astounded her. His mother was Irish but not his father. That much he did learn because of his mother's Irish accent. 'I'm Oirish, Oirish!' she had told copious people in his hearing as a young boy. People sometimes mistook, in their ignorance, her for Scottish. 'Now do I sound, Scattish? Oirish, Oirish! You'll all have to go for Oirish electrocution lessons to get it right, to be sure. You'll never get it wrong again.' She always laughed at her own jokes and clearly mockery was her partner in chit chat.

'Now you have it,' her father had answered, 'It's all I know. As for anymore questions, I don't know the answer, so please don't ask.'

'Hello Paula,' greeted Thomas, 'I didn't notice you there. Do feel at home.'

'Hello Thomas.' She was at a loss for further words after recalling those words of her father.

'So Thomas, I would love to go to Paula's for the afternoon. I haven't been for a long time. She invited me for some sister time; a rare thing for us just to enjoy one another.'

Thomas had been enjoying his own company and much needed space. Their presence, and even Beverly's own presence, antagonized him when thinking deeply but on this occasion he found Paula's presence a Godsend. 'It's no problem to have you here this afternoon, both of you. You can spend time together here, in the lounge. Have tea, walk in the garden, play tiddlywinks, whatever.'

'That's kind of you, Thomas, but I need to get ready for an exam and my time is kind of restricted and to stay for so long would hamper my studies. That's the real reason Beverly is coming, to help me with the exam.'

64

'Why didn't you tell me, Beverly? Well, you must come back here one day, Paula, and enjoy dinner with us.'

'Thank you. I would love to.'

Exchanging smiles the two ladies turned their backs and arm in arm headed towards the front door. Thomas stared at their backs, especially Paula's, and wondered when he could interrogate her about the journal.

Once clear of the house, Beverly cheered, 'Good one, Paula, I'd never have thought of that.'

'It's good to pray, Beverly. It's good to pray; God surprises us sometimes. Remember what happened when I prayed for God's help for Sidney?'

'Well, something answers you, Paula, that's for sure.'

On arrival at her dainty and ordered abode and having led Beverly to her lounge, Paula headed directly to her small kitchen where she removed two chunky mugs by their rather large handles from the cupboard, placed them on a tray and then put the kettle on. Beverly loved her cups of tea. Stress always beckoned a mug or two. It was the same reason as when her father smoked his never ending cigarettes. Tea was healthier.

'Chocolate cake?' Paula shouted from the kitchen.

Beverly turned her head away from the window where she was watching a horse grazing in the fields opposite,

'Please.'

Paula cut two generous slices.

'Much needed sister time.' Beverly continued, smiling. 'Tell me more about your life with dad. Thomas won't be expecting me back for a couple of hours. He starts cooking at five when he's home. That's another thing he loves to do, besides the garden.'

'You're lucky, Beverly.'

'If you think so, Paula, to you I'm lucky.'

'I'm grateful for what I have though, at least I'm safe,' said Paula while carrying the much needed treat out of the kitchen. They sat side by side on the two seater settee and helped themselves then after enjoying the change of atmosphere they ate and drank in peace and quiet. Once refreshed Paula removed the tray while wondering what to say to her sister regarding her time at home with her dad. As she emerged from the kitchen and back to her seat Beverly said, 'I'm ready. We've got about an hour left.'

Paula glanced at her watch and began,

'Dad, after Sidney left, became terribly depressed. No matter what I did for him, though there was never any communication except the ordinary things in life, he just never picked up. At times he seemed so sad, so forlorn, that my heart went out to him but I knew it was useless. At times he would surface but only to rage at me. Screaming that I was the most useless daughter anyone could imagine having. Then he would sob. But he managed to work okay, at his work, you know. An electrician's work always sees sparks flying; he must have taken after his mum and her electrocution joke.'

'What joke is that?'

She explained to Beverly about the Irish roots.'

Beverly surmised, 'That's possibly why he became an electrician then; possibly the only thing that connected him to anything meaningful in life, especially losing his family in that way. That's amazing we have Irish roots. I wonder how she came to be over here.'

'Yeah, I often wonder how we came to evolve to this place. I was dreading living with dad on my own; couldn't wait for my sixteenth birthday. After that incident towards Sidney I saw a side in him that I had never seen emerge since we were young. What on earth happened? Well, of course we know what happened to make him so angry but to hate his own children… that's what gets me.'

Beverly shifted to sit on Paula's bean bag so she could face her, 'How did he treat you?'

'For one thing I had to keep myself going. Getting ready for school, doing homework when I got back, getting his stuff ready for the next day and stuff like that. It was really scary when I needed money because he didn't have any spare to give me so he just shouted and screamed at me instead. I had to get small jobs behind his back now and again but kept having to leave them because I wasn't getting the house ship shape enough. I was really missing you, Carl and Sidney and often

I lay alone at night thinking of you all and cried myself to sleep. Sometimes Sidney came over on his days off and helped a bit. Dad loved it when he came. Dad's soft spot, but it was only for Sidney. I'm pretty sure he knew just how much he had sunk that night.

'One night as I lay awake on that worn out bed, I wondered about trying to talk to him; at least to try for a smile for myself. When I asked for anything he merely told me how selfish I was but he only had me to cater for, didn't he? It got me down so much and I became so depressed that my teacher asked me what the matter was. I told her about dad. She said she understood but I doubt that she did. She said she would lighten pressure on homework but I needed the study or how would I get on when I left home? How would I get a good job?

'When Father's Day came around I wondered what I could do for him that I wasn't already doing. Next time Sidney came I invited him to come around on Father's Day and I would cook a special meal with whatever we had. Sidney said okay and he must have told the farmer because he came round with all sorts of food. I never had to trouble myself with the cooking even. There was cold roast lamb, all kinds of other meats, scraps really but great for us and then rolls with real butter made at the farm and salad and a fruit trifle the farmer's wife had prepared. Honestly, we couldn't have done better. Dad merely accepted it with no emotion. It was only when he saw the farmer waving bye to Sidney that he realized it was all a gift and not from me. I mean, how on earth could it have been from me? The thought was from me or he wouldn't have tasted a thing and maybe he knew that much and was rejecting even that thought. I ate with them but he only spoke to and looked at Sidney. But Sidney never responded much to him. His just being there was a medicine for dad. It must have been the forgiveness. Dad knew he had broken Sidney beyond repair but I could tell Sidney loved dad. He wouldn't have come otherwise. That's what children do isn't it? Love through thick and thin.'

'Did the farmer come into the house?' asked Beverly, leaning forward with her face cupped in her hands, concentrating.

'No, he drew up in an old banger and handed the food to me and Sidney so when dad saw the farmer waving he gave a short wave, a quick nod and looked down towards his shoes; like he was ashamed or something. He had every right to be ashamed really, treating us the way he did, didn't he?'

'Yes, very much so.'

'I did feel a bit ashamed myself because I had wanted to cook something. It's like my thought was stolen from me and it could well have been that dad thought it was all Sidney's doing, who knows. I just sat and listened to dad asking Sidney about the farm, what his favourite animals were and things like that. Then dad left the room, went upstairs and when he came back he had a photograph with him. A smile crept across both his and Sidney's face as dad showed him a bear cub rolling around on the deck of a ship with sailors playing with it. I might as well not have been in the room or even in the house for that matter so straight after dinner I left the room.'

'Leaving Sidney with dad, alone?' Beverly sat up, horrified.

'Yep. I went to my room and never came out for the rest of the day. They didn't miss me at all. Sidney never said goodbye when he left and just before I heard dad close the door he said to Sidney, "see ya mate: like he was talking to an old sailor buddy. Sidney managed a word or two as I heard quite clearly, "aye, aye, Skipper."

Dad must have told him some stories about his life in the Navy. Sidney never told me anything about that day. My heart was broken, my own family ostracizing me.'

'Carl and I didn't ostracize you. We just never wanted to come home again. We wanted to get on with our lives but I never stopped thinking about you. Not one day went by when I didn't wonder what was going on.'

'The journal will tell everything from dad's side of things, it must. I'm glad he has gone. But he isn't gone because what he has done to me and you, Carl and Sidney stays with us. We have to somehow make the most, or should I say the least, of what he handed down to us. Your Thomas seems a nice bloke. A good husband, well, better than dad anyway.'

'He's not cruel, if that's what you mean but he seems pretty spoiled to me. I go along with it because I can't cope with too much stress.'

'I don't blame you. The less stress the better. Would you like a glass of water or more tea? I'm getting thirsty.'

'Half a glass of water would be good, thanks.'

Paula poured two glasses from the kitchen tap after letting it run cold for a few seconds.

'Should we invite Sidney round one time? We could try to help him a bit,' shouted Beverly.

'Well, it's a thought,' answered Paula, while handing Beverly her glass.

'We'll have to think about that as it might be a bit of a struggle. It may work, it may not. Let's read the journal first. It might help us understand him more.' Beverly pulled up her sleeve to check her watch.

'It's twenty to five. I better get going.' She placed her glass on the coffee table and thanking Paula for the afternoon, made her way to the front door. 'We'll sort you illness out next,' she laughed.

১

Thomas had been waiting for Beverly to return before he dished up the supper. Fish and chips never took long if one of them was out so that's what they ate. Thomas lay his chips in two slices of bread and butter and watched the butter melt to a liquid. As it soaked the bread he found no words for his wife who merely dipped hers in tomato sauce.

'So,' he said at last with a full mouth, 'how did you get on with Paula?'

'It was a much needed time.'

'Study, how did the study go?'

'Actually she wasn't feeling too well so had to skip that. We just talked.'

'She seemed fine when she was here.' He lifted the bread from his chips to scatter more salt on. Replacing it he leant forwards to suggest that Paula come over for a meal this week.

'Ring and ask her.'

'No.'

'What?'

'No, I want to plan it first. Then I will ask when I'm good and ready.'

'Okay.' Beverly cleared the plates to wash up. Thomas brought out two individual apple pies he had heated in the oven.

'Sit down and eat this before you wash up. Save your energy.'

'Right.' Beverly sat back down.

'So Paula's not well.'

'She should be fine in a day or two. I think it's the stress of having to face so many issues with dad dying.'

'Quite.'

A tense silence followed and prevailed throughout the rest of the evening as both of them grappled with their circumstances and how to overcome them; Thomas in the gym and Beverly sat alone trying to take her mind off things by reading in the lounge but lack of concentration held her on the same page for a couple of hours At least it covered the fact that she had so much on her mind. Thomas wouldn't notice anyway, whatever she was doing. Finally, she made her way upstairs to get ready for an early night, took up another book and pretended to read again. As soon as Thomas came into the bedroom from his evening ritual and watching the ten o'clock news she closed the book, put it back on her locker, lay down and closed her eyes. When she reopened them the night had passed. She wondered what the day would bring, any more surprises, any more stress?

Thomas rose first and said he would make his own breakfast, leaving Beverly to get her own. At times that was the best way forward to avoid any confrontations. It had become second nature to them.

Beverly waited for him to leave the house then attended to her own needs before leaving for another day's sorting. By three o'clock she had done enough and left what remained until Saturday for Paula to come and help. She moved one of the filled and closed boxes in the kitchen in front of the dresser doors, sat on it and rested her head against one of them. The kettle summoned her but she felt too exhausted to lift it. Making her way into the lounge for a more comfortable rest she lay on the shabby settee, put the thin blanket that draped the back of it over her and allowed the tension to drain slowly away. About half an hour later when her body felt rejuvenated she gathered her belongings and made her way home. Thomas's car sat in the drive signaling he was home. She wondered about his mood as she opened the front door. The clatter of utensils drew her to investigate what he was up to in the kitchen.

'Roast beef and Yorkshire pudding,' he announced, before she could ask the question about what was for dinner. 'You better be hungry because we are going to dine well tonight.'

So the morning's tension had passed away too. Beverly wondered why. 'It sounds absolutely wonderful, thank you.' She dropped her coat and bag on the counter. He turned from the sink to enquire of the sound,

'Can you hang those up, please; I want to set our places. I bumped into Paula at the hospital; she'll be over as soon as she has changed,' he slid the beef into the preheated oven. 'She'll be coming in about half an hour.'

'Paula, isn't she busy? Doesn't she want to study?' As she dragged her belongings from the counter she wondered what else he could have said to her. Pegging her coat and bag back on the hall pegs she perused how she could talk to Paula before the meal. There would be no way for her to remind her not to say a word about the journal in front of Thomas.

'Not tonight, I persuaded her to leave everything and to relax here before going home to study,' he answered, raising his voice.

'I'm going up to change.' Beverly nipped upstairs, checked the time, then slipped into a casual skirt and jumper. So, Paula would be here in about twenty minutes. Beverly scribbled a note then quietly put it into her skirt pocket. On the way back downstairs she breathed in the gentle aroma of the beef heating up.

'Can I do anything?' she asked on entering the kitchen.

'No, I would rather do it all by myself,' he said proudly. 'Your sister is quite a nurse you know and deserves to be praised. I will take that honour this evening.' he peeled one of his best potatoes and cut it into quarters then put them into a pan to parboil before roasting.

'Where did you learn to cook, Thomas?' Beverly asked as he cut the carrots in uniform slices at the speed of a professional, 'and how come you love it so much?'

'Boarding school,' he answered abruptly.

Time seemed to stand still while waiting for Paula's arrival. Beverly leaned against the breakfast counter while checking on the front door every few seconds. Thomas had his hands full so he would not be answering it.

'I'll go and sit in the lounge.'

'Great, let your sister in when she comes, please.'

As if I wouldn't, she thought. Barely had she arrived at the lounge door when the familiar figure's outline appeared behind the frosted glass door. Beverly silently removed the scribbled on piece of paper from her pocket and opened it with one hand while turning the front door knob with the other. Not giving her sister a chance to say a word in hello she held up the note.

'What's that?' Paula asked aloud.

Beverly quickly put a finger to her lips, the only sign language she knew.

'Sorry,' whispered Paula, 'okay, got it.'

Beverly slipped the paper back into her pocket and greeted her sister in the normal fashion for Thomas's benefit. Paula, dressed smartly in her long emerald pleated skirt and yellow cardigan, hung her coat on the peg then walking arm in arm towards the kitchen with Beverly confidently praising Thomas on the aroma of his succulent smelling roast beef. Thomas turned just as they entered through the door.

'What a wonderful set up,' proclaimed Paula, 'I bet you are as proud as punch of your husband aren't you, Beverly?'

'Naturally,' she winked at her sister as Thomas turned his back, 'you'll have one of your own one day.'

'I doubt it.'

'Make yourself comfortable, Paula,' invited Thomas, looking around again.

'Thank you.'

'I'll take her into the lounge until you are ready. Just give us a shout.'

Once seated in her favourite chair Beverly asked, 'How's your day been then, Paula?'

'Certainly surprising as you can see. I didn't for one minute expect to get an invitation to your house in such circumstances. Does my hair look alright?'

'Your hair's lovely as always. Where did you meet him?'

'He was walking up the ward, I was working on it for about an hour and in he comes to do a ward round. I was the one who took him round. He said to the Sister that he would like me to help him so I could get some experience. I think I went bright red, actually. Am I red now?'

'You're always slightly flushed when you're busy so I doubt if anyone noticed. You're a little flushed but nothing out of the ordinary. Did the Sister accompany you?'

'At first but when she saw I knew the patients well she left to get on with writing her reports.'

'How did he get to invite you to supper?'

'After we finished he and Sister were really flattering me on my performance. He told her I was his sister-in-law and that he'd a good mind to invite me for dinner to reward me – re ward me. I wonder if he meant the pun.'

'No, it's your quick wit.'

'So, here I am, feeling very happy to be found worthy.'

Thomas shouted, 'Okay, dinner's done, your chef is calling.'

As they stood Beverly again put her finger to her lips. Paula nodded.

The sisters stood perfectly still when they encountered the spread on the counter.

'Well, both of you, don't just stand there. Take a seat.'

Beverly had never seen such a spread in her two or three years of marriage. 'I am so impressed. Just look at those Yorkshire puddings, sprouts, carrots, everything, horseradish sauce, the lot.'

'Glass of wine?' He held up the bottle in true butler style, poured some into a glass, swilled it around, took a sniff and generally made the sisters laugh. When all glasses were full and Thomas had handed the food around for them to help themselves, Thomas proposed a toast to the 'best nurse in the universe'. Beverly found the change in him quite romantic and so did Paula. 'Eat up or it'll go cold.'

When the wine had been drunk to the half way mark, Thomas began to speak.

'So, Paula, how's the sorting going in your father's house? I hear you've been busy helping Beverly. You're a darn good worker, I'll give you that.'

Beverly side kicked Paula gently to remind her again not to say a word.

'I haven't been at the house all week as I've been on duty. We got quite a bit done before that. On Friday I'm working again but this weekend we'll be back.'

'This clearing up business after a death, it's pretty depressing, don't you think?' Thomas declared after finishing chewing a mouthful of tender beef. He cut one of his crisp, brown potatoes while waiting for a response.

'Well, it can be but to tell you the truth when we are so busy with what's what and packing things into boxes time goes pretty fast and we don't have time to get bogged down. But yes, if you stop to have a break the atmosphere can become a bit morose, especially in a house as poor as our father's.' Paula lifted her glass, quickly glanced at Thomas, then shifted her gaze to the garden on her left.

'You've got a great garden out there, Thomas, as well as a great cook, you are one amazing gardener.'

'You can't see it right now, being dark, but yes, it's my best hobby. I wouldn't change my life for the world. '

'So Paula, where's…?' he stopped to take a gulp of wine.

Paula gave him her full attention, 'Where's what?'

Thomas stared for a while into the steam rising from the gravy boat, distracting himself from her innocent expression. *Where's what?* He repeated to himself while taking another couple of mouthfuls of wine. Beverly watched her husband acting in a way she had never seen. She looked away in embarrassment.

'Haven't you had enough wine?' asked Beverly.

74

Thomas raised his eyebrows as if to say, 'What are you talking about?' Then he addressed Paula, 'I was going to ask you. Did your dad leave anything of value to any of you, if you don't mind me asking? Remember Carl had found a bit of paper with that, what was it, something about getting rid of somebody but, of course, I don't mean stuff like that, happy things, you know. It's always nice to find stuff like, well, of sentimental value. There didn't seem to be much in the way of material value in the house when I went with Beverly, did there, Bev?'

'No, just a few Navy medals and things like that that I found with Paula the other day.'

'Do have more wine, Paula,' pressed Thomas.

'No thank you, I'm driving, remember and you may well have a hangover tomorrow.'

'Not me. Well, how about a dessert now that we've all finished our first course?' Thomas offered while Beverly stacked the plates.

'That would be most welcome. What is it?'

'Sherry trifle, with plenty of sherry. It's okay; it won't hurt to have it in trifle.' Thomas tried to keep his mood up and not to show signs of disappointment at not being able to draw anything out of Paula regarding the journal but he wouldn't give up. It's early days yet and confidence has to be earned. 'Please can you bring the trifle from the fridge, Beverly and the dishes?' he asked slightly slurring his words. It was obvious to Beverly that he was not used to drinking alcohol.

'Now Paula, do you read and what kind of books do you like?'

Paula thought of the most recent book she had read, her father's journal,

'I love autobiographies and any true stories. They make a nice change from study books.'

Beverly quickly crossed back with the trifle then hurried to bring the crystal dishes from the cabinet in the lounge. As she passed behind Thomas she waved frantically at Paula and once her attention was gained put a finger to her lips. Her heart pounded so hard she could swear Thomas would have detected it even without a stethoscope. She wiped her forehead. On her return with the dishes she discovered

Thomas had moved to sit next to Paula, rather than opposite. Bad move, thought Beverly, my sister hates men being that close to her.

'Here's the dishes, Thomas,' she plonked them down in his place, 'are you going to dish up?'

Paula stared at her sister with the familiar expression of fear on her face, pleading to be rescued.

Thomas reluctantly moved back to his place to dish up the dessert. He wanted to ask Paula outright about the journal but Beverly's return ruined his plans.

'How much would you like, Paula? Guests first.'

'Not too much, thank you. I'm already full but it looks delicious.'

'We were talking about books,' Thomas continued, 'I love to read autobiographies too and I may even write one some day. Not that my life has been interesting but it might interest some people. Have either of your written any diaries or journals?'

'No,' Beverly and Paula answered together.

'We'd rather forget our history, thank you, Thomas,' Beverly said, 'not having a good life doesn't make for great reading. Unless, or course, somebody would like to know about abuse and things like that.'

Thomas, rather embarrassed at the rebuke, dug his spoon into his trifle, withdrawing it piled high and shoved the entire spoonful into his mouth. *Why don't you just shut up?*

'Some people like to hear about good outcomes in some stories. Where there are good ones, they are the best kind, to bring hope.' Paula suggested boldly.

Thomas tried again, 'Does any of your family like to write about their lives? How about your dad, he had an interesting life in the Navy, didn't he?'

Beverly swept his question aside, 'He wasn't the type to write though. He was always too morose. I can't imagine him putting pen to paper. Never did he say a word about his life to any of us, let alone write about it.'

Paula rested her elbows on the table, 'Why do you ask, Thomas?'

Thomas, feeling slightly tipsy, came to the conclusion that he get nowhere with this conversation so toyed with another idea. He answered Paula, 'Just small talk over dinner. Let's finish up then, you must be tired.' At least he had discovered neither of them knew anything about a journal but just in case they were bluffing he would use Sidney to investigate, undercover. Before that he would give it one more try while Paula was in his house, 'How about a coffee before you leave Paula? Beverly, would you do the honours, please?'

'Sure.'

Thomas had already consumed at least two glasses of wine to loosen his tongue. He sidled back over to Paula's side of the counter. Seated on Beverly's stool he reached out towards her. His arm hung loosely across her shoulder. Paula froze in her seat. Unable to move even her tongue in protest, she waited. Thomas misunderstood her body language. His arm remained where it was until Beverly turned to notice what he had done. Her sister had turned white with shock. Beverly hurried over to Thomas and removed his arm from where it had rested. She quickly returned for the drinks and ordered Thomas back to his place. Paula sat unable to lift her cup to her lips. Beverly stayed beside her and tried to coax her out of the trance she had fallen into. 'Thomas, this is what abuse does to someone. That was rather insensitive of you. Please don't do it again. It has obviously reminded Paula of something traumatic. Please apologize.'

Thomas had never witnessed such a reaction in his life and so apologized. Beverly remembered Paula's reaction to Sidney that awful night so remained beside her sister until she resurfaced. Paula's coffee, not cold, was left untouched when she asked Beverly walk her to her car. Beverly fetched Paula's coat from the hall and after Paula nodded towards Thomas, accepting his apology, the sisters made their way to the front door. Paula turned to shout a feeble thank you and goodbye to Thomas. Beverly watched Paula as she drove out of the drive and disappear into the lane. On Beverly's return to the house Thomas's silence resumed. She stated how embarrassed she was at his approach regarding any journal.

'Sorry, Bev, I must be drunk. Drink brings all kinds of stuff out of a person. I must have imagined it.' Following that event, even in his drunken state, he had the ability to realize he had divulged what he knew about the journal.

'Yes, you must have. I'll make you a strong black coffee; that will sober you up. Try to forget about it. You need to have a workout when you've finished it in case the trifle settles in your arteries,'

'I simply cannot exercise with trifle clinging to my arteries.'

Beverly laughed, 'I hope Paula will be alright after what you did.' She turned her head in his direction after nodding towards where Paula had been sitting. Leaving her seat to fill the kettle again she left Thomas to think things through. After making the hot drinks and setting Thomas's in front of him Beverly carried her mug of strong white coffee into the lounge. To distract herself from the shock of the disastrous evening she leaned forward to pick up the local newspaper to leaf through to the daily crossword puzzle. After solving two clues she rested the pencil and paper back on the table and, feeling frustrated, made her way upstairs. She found Thomas's gym clothes and made for the kitchen with them. Dumping them over his arm as he sat at the counter she said,

'I'm sure you feel like a workout now. Have a go.'

Walking away from him she took to the stairs once again.

Thomas pushed the clothes off and slightly swaying walked to the lounge, lay on the settee then breathed deeply until he fell asleep. By ten o'clock he had not made his way up to bed. Beverly shrugged her shoulders and left him to it. If he smells of alcohol tomorrow so be it. She had done her best. She picked up her book but her appetite for words had vanished so she rested her head on back on the pillow. Thomas can wake up with his hangover on his own. Enjoying the entire bed to herself she fell asleep. In the morning she spread her arms wide and focused on the peace being alone had brought her. Checking the clock she swung her legs out of the bed and made her way down the stairs to check on Thomas. He was still fast sleep.

'Thomas,' she whispered loudly, 'Thomas, you must get up and ready for work. It's almost eight.' She shook him until he stirred and groaned. 'Come on, hurry up. I'll get your breakfast but you get upstairs, washed and dressed.'

'What, what am I doing here?' he whimpered.

'Never mind, just get up now.'

The day passed without any further surprises. Thomas must have sobered up in the atmosphere of work pretty sharply once there.

Beverly spent the day touring the Royal Navy Base. It had been a spur of the moment decision and after Thomas left for work. She wanted to taste a glimpse of what her father would have experienced on a daily basis, if at all possible. On her arrival around eleven o'clock she made her way towards the first ship she laid eyes on. Sailors in uniform greeted her with a salute and smile then whispered, whistled and laughed as she passed by. No matter, she carried on to the quayside. While standing beside the huge vessel, amidst all the noise, she tried to imagine her father at sixteen years of age running around and feeling rather lost in such a huge establishment. She smelled the sea air and imagined the war years on board one of these enormous ships. Not that she knew anything about the war and certainly did not know anything about the Royal Navy. The years shaped him, the Navy shaped him and 'her' shaped him into what he had become the day he died. Her mother, a bright spark of love was all that he encountered with any positive feeling. With each baby born they equally brought him a sense of great delight. But those were short years in comparison to his suffering ones. She turned to where some sailors busied themselves carrying ropes and other equipment. Her dad was once somebody like that. They were all down here years ago and none of them could imagine that one day one of his daughters would stand and remember them. She tried, but failed, to materialize and speak to them. Time could not be medaled with except when winding a watch or clock backwards or forwards by only, at the most, a full twelve hours.

'Can I help you, Ma'am?' an unfamiliar voice asked from behind.

She turned to face a kind looking Captain. Her heart missed a beat,' Err, no, I... I'm just here on a family thing. My father used to work here, live here even, at HMS Pembroke in the barracks. He has recently died and I'm trying to find out what life must have been like for him.'

The Captain removed his hat out of courtesy and scratched his head. 'HMS Pembroke is across the road, Ma'am. You are at the Dockyard. Do you mind me asking his name?'

'Not at all, his name was Ralph Hopkins.'

'It doesn't ring a bell.' He said after scouring his memory for a few seconds.

'No, too many years have passed for anyone to remember his being a sailor, thank you, anyway. I appreciate you asking but I am fine if I may wander around the place.'

'I can show you, if you like, or get someone else.'

'Maybe I will come down with my sister and we can do a tour together? My two brothers may want to as well. It can't have been a comfortable life.'

'Fighting is never about comfort for the moment but only for something to look forward to once it's over. You can contact me any time when you are ready and I'll see what I can do to give you the tour.'

'Thank you, I'll remember that. Could I please have your name?' She reached into her bag to find a pen and note book.

'Captain Murphy, Ma'am. I'm happy to have met you.'

'I won't be long here as I have shopping to do later.' She replaced her pen and book then closed her bag tight.

'You're welcome, Ma'am.'

Beverly turned away from the ship and made her way towards a huge hangar which looked as if it made chains but the noise was too deafening to stay. She decided to leave looking around until Paula could accompany her. In her vulnerability and all at once self consciousness she walked quickly passed men and women milling around the courtyard and left the premises. The Captain kept his eye on her until she reached the gate, guessing she had changed her mind about a self made tour. At the gate she turned, not expecting to still see him standing where she had stood to take in her father's life. He replaced his hat and, without any further gesture, marched away.

She took the bus into Chatham to buy food and various other items and then picked up her car where she had left it at a safe parking spot not too far from the shopping centre. She would soon be home and this evening she would bake a few cakes to take to her father's house for her and Paula to enjoy. At four o'clock she unpacked her shopping hoping Thomas did not mind what she had bought. There was nothing unusual but the additional ingredients for the cakes, which were not meant for him but, no doubt, he would want a few. When he arrived at five she already had them in the oven and was just about to leave the kitchen to go upstairs when he entered the house.

'Hi,' she said and nothing else.

He carried on to investigate the smell without as much as a hi in return. 'What are you cooking?' he shouted as he returned to the hall to hang up his coat.

'A few cakes for Paula and me.'

'I can't hear you properly, come down and tell me.'

Beverly watered a few plants in the bathroom before descending to face the evening with him. He would see it was cakes if he looked but nevertheless, she answered his call to come down after removing some dead leaves from the African Violet. She admired the deep purple flower and contrasting yellow anthers. On reaching the kitchen Thomas had already rolled his sleeves up and had started to prepare the supper.

'I've taken the cakes out of the oven. They're just about done.'

'Thanks, Thomas. Would you like one?'

'What did you say upstairs?'

'I said they were cakes for Paula and me when we are at our dad's house but you're welcome to one.'

'Or two,' he said flatly.

'How has your day been?' Beverly asked.

'Not too bad but those patients are a bit testing at times.'

'I know. Would you like a cup of tea or do you want to wait till after dinner?' asked Beverly while placing the cakes on a cooking tray.

'I'll have one now please, this will be another half hour yet or so. When it's done take yours to the lounge. I'll drink mine here.'

Beverly was glad to put her feet up after her day out. Thomas never or rarely asked her about her day, assuming nothing exciting ever happened to her. She would not offer news of the events either. As she sat with her tea in the lounge she concentrated on the grandfather clock for a bit but as there was no shadow it only appeared a dull instrument of time passing so she turned her thoughts back to her meeting with Captain Murphy. She would definitely mention him to Paula at the weekend and then to her brothers in due course. She sat until her tea was finished, which wasn't long and then watered the other houseplants around the house. If any drooped there would be trouble, so none ever did.

As she returned to the kitchen to check that her cakes were cool enough to store Thomas asked her to set the counter.

'As soon as I've put these away.'

Before she could say another word, Thomas grabbed the cutlery drawer and removed the knives, forks and spoons. Beverly took them from him and, ignoring the cakes, she placed them on the counter. First things always first, Thomas, that's what's first! Then she put the cakes away.

Once sitting to the meal Beverly sat deep in thought as she ate the shepherd's pie Thomas had made.

'So, how's Paula?' he asked, twirling his fork in mid air.

'Pardon?'

'How's Paula? Is she coping with your dad's death?'

'She's glad he's gone to tell you the truth. She isn't feeling too good though, Thomas. I have to keep an eye on her. She is very tired and feeling quite under par these days. I told her to go to the doctor, to get her blood tested. She could be anaemic or something. We are meeting up again tomorrow to get more sorting done. I'll see if she has made an appointment then.'

He laid his fork on top of a mound of mashed potato then picked up his knife, which had lain clean beside his plate until he chose to pick it up for cutting his cauliflower.

'Okay, so after an appointment and she is checked the doctor will let her know.'

'That will be, maybe next week, towards the end.'

'Perhaps I could see her off the record, Beverly. I can usually tell what somebody has wrong with them and may be able to give my diagnosis and you can see if her doctor confirms it.' He took firmer grip of both knife and fork, sat bolt upright and ate his meal with a zeal Beverly had not seen in a long time and wondered if he was cooking up some kind of idea.

'Paula is a very private person. She doesn't discuss personal health outside her own doctor. She will tell me only if things are serious.'

'So, who is her doctor?'

'I have no idea. She does not discuss even that with me.'

'No?'

'Nup. She only lets them know who her next of kin are but only for the doctor to contact them should things be absolutely necessary.'

'It's a bit strange that, isn't it?'

'What?'

'Not to tell you.'

'I think that too, but it's how she wants it. It was the last year she spent with dad on her own. She lost all confidence in people and keeps everything under wraps, to protect herself.'

Thomas ate slower and, once finished, set his plate aside. With his plans foiled he had to think up some other way to get to Paula.

'So, how's Sidney? Is he still working at the farm? He's been there for many years now. What does he do with his spare time?'

'Who knows but I think he relaxes with his pets. He had two dogs last time I knew of anything.'

Thomas's eyes shifted towards the left, then towards the right and then directly at Beverly.

'Beverly, you look tired. Why not go for an early night. I can do the dishes and then I have to go out for some petrol.'

'I think I will. It's been full on and I should be refreshed for tomorrow.'

'Are you almost finished?'

'Yes, shouldn't be too long now. Thank you, Thomas, for considering me.'

She pushed her plate towards him and turned away from the breakfast counter.

'That's okay, Beverly, see you later.'

Much later, he thought. She kissed him gently on the cheek and rubbed his back as she passed by. He warmed to her touch and all at once twisted his body to leave his stool. Standing in front of her, he softened his voice and spoke quite tenderly,

'Beverly, before you go, oh never mind.'

He came back to his senses and returned to the coolness of his emotions. He must not allow himself to melt towards her. Love was not for him. He remembered bonding only leads to pain, much pain, besides he was her half brother so ought not to be so familiar with her as to keep this marriage beyond what it was designed for. His mother would not approve and neither would Beverly if she was ever to find out the truth. How could he break away from such a union when his mother demanded what she did? She would not leave his side, figuratively speaking, until the children were all destroyed, completely destroyed. Thomas, her spy, would find the journal and in all loyalty to his mother he would never lie to her. She had ways of finding out everything.

'During the requiem Mass Thomas had made his way, early that morning, to tell her the news he had discovered. She did not want to be seen with him anywhere. Moments later she dressed herself to the hilt in black and after Thomas drove her to within walking distance of the church she braced herself, took a deep breath and performed her duties towards the man who had given her a son and all she ever wanted. She had laid her bouquet so quickly, with that air of confidence and authority that would give the family something to ponder over for weeks, months or years. However long it took for Thomas to find the journal he would get no rest. Why couldn't he just have kept his mouth shut; kept the journal a secret, not involved her at all? Such habits of loyalty were hard to break. She insisted that if he didn't find it she knew somebody who would. That would spell trouble for him and his household for sure. He didn't want somebody prying around his affairs, searching his home or anything of that nature. He would do it himself and when he found it he would, in his loyalty, give it to his mother. Ralph's children would never find out about their father's love for them if he could help it. One of them and possibly two, whoever had the journal would know about the father's love, his life, and whatever else it held inside. As yet not one had shown any sign of knowing anything which signified that it had not yet been read. He must act quickly.

'Leaving Beverly in the comfort of her early night he left the house for the petrol, leaving the washing up till later. Driving past familiar roads of Gillingham, he made his way along the London Road towards the Sittingbourne farm where Sidney worked. Pulling up outside the quaint farmhouse he switched off the engine and sat for a while pondering what he would say. Somebody passed a window indoors as dogs barked and growled. A rough looking man he presumed was the farmer opened the front door to quieten the dogs. Thomas wound down the window as the farmer shouted,

'Hello, can I help you?'

In the dark yet early evening he opened the car door an inch or two. Bits of straw and dirt covering the gravel path were scattered around by the dogs scampering feet. He waited until the dogs were taken inside before opening the car door fully. On his return the farmer peered at Thomas inquisitively.

'I've come to see Sidney on urgent business,' Thomas explained hurriedly from the car. 'My name is Thomas and I am here on behalf of Beverly, Sidney's sister. I'm her husband. She wants to ask him a favour but is stuck at home with the flu and cannot come herself.'

'I'm Mr Feathergill, you better come on in, the dogs are in an outhouse so can't do any harm.'

'Thank you for the rescue,' Thomas said as he left the car, crossed the forecourt and hurried into the house.

'I'll call Sidney, just wait there. He's in the back field feeding the pigs.'

Sidney put down the pig swill in answer to Mr Feathergill and, as pungent as he smelt, made his way into the house to face Thomas. Thomas turned his nose away but that was all. He had something to do and would not leave, no matter, until he had done it.

'Sidney, Beverly is ill with the flu and has asked me to ask you a favour.'

'Sure, if I can,' he glanced towards Mr Feathergill for permission, if necessary. His innocence had not changed; neither had his tough physique waned. Of course in those funeral clothes he had been covered up. The cold never bothered him. Autumn air inspired him to work harder to keep warm. He faced Thomas with his shirt sleeves rolled up to his elbows. Thomas, happy that Sidney was a simple type; not violent or bad tempered; reached a friendly arm towards him. He was easy to manipulate or he would be no match should he have met an angry Sidney.

'Do you have any spare time? Beverly wants to know if you could visit Paula as soon as possible. Paula has a book that belonged to your dad. It's a journal he wrote which cannot be found.'

'She wants it now? But I smell of pigs.'

'I can vouch for that. You could get a wash and come as soon as you can. I will drive you to Paula's and give you ten minutes to ask her about it. Don't say I said so as it's Beverly who wants it. I will wait in the car outside You mustn't even mention my name.'

Sidney took off to change but the smell of pigs could not be washed away completely. It was not long before he joined Thomas. 'Is that better? At least I smell of soap now.'

'Well, just about,' smiled Thomas.

Thomas suffered in silence all the way to Paula's in Upchurch. Sidney gave Thomas copious glances and wondered why he did not want to be mentioned by name. He might be simple but he wasn't stupid. He might be quiet but he knew a trick when he saw one. Pigs will eat anything but not Sidney. He was a deep thinker but rarely shared his thoughts with anybody, except on occasions his dogs.

'I'll do as you say,' he could match any bluff.

Thomas drew to a halt out of sight from Paula's flat. As Sidney stepped from the car Thomas stressed,

'Remember; don't mention my name at all.'

Sidney found the flat without any trouble. He had been there a couple of times with the farmer to help her move in. He remembered her blue door with the lion face knocker and number five above, in brass. The door led to a hall whose steps, in turn, led to the first floor flat. He sniffed himself for pig fragrance and straightened his jacket then ran a hand over his eye level fringe, moving it from his view. As he waited for her response he turned to where the car was parked. Thomas's head was just about visible. He had less than ten minutes. He knocked again before bearing his right wrist to look at the time; seven thirty. A female's shadow emerged from the hall and he grew slightly nervous. Paula shouted through the closed door,

'Who is it?'

'Sidney, your brother, Beverly has sent me.'

Paula opened the door and, slightly taken aback at the faint pong, did not open it too wide.

'Beverly sent you? But she was just here a couple of hours ago. Has something happened?'

'She has flu.'

'In two hours since she left? She was fine. How did you get here?'

'Thomas came to the farm to tell me and…'

'Thomas? Where is he?'

'He told me not to tell you.'

'You better come in then but you really need a bath.'

'I know.' As he followed her up the stairs he explained. 'I was feeding the pigs but Thomas says this is urgent. He said not to mention him so please don't tell him I told you.'

Paula pushed open the door to her flat, 'Come in but don't sit down. You need that bath first.'

'I can't have a bath here. I have less than ten minutes to tell you then have to go.'

'What does Beverly want?' Paula asked, facing him.

'She wants a book.'

'A book?'

'Yes, it's a journal. Thomas says you have it. It belongs to dad.'

'I don't have any book of dad's, none whatsoever. What makes Beverly think I have it?'

'I don't know, Thomas just gave me Beverly's message.'

Paula recalled Beverly's instructions not to tell no matter what, even if Thomas says anything more. Both she and Beverly continued to hold tight as to its whereabouts. Her cheeks flushed slightly. She turned towards the kitchen sink to get herself a glass of water. 'Go and tell Thomas quickly that I don't have such a book.'

'I can't, he'll know I've mentioned his name if I do.'

'Okay. I tell you what, you search the place and if you find such a journal take it with you, if not you can't take it, simple as that.'

Sidney felt thoroughly awkward and refused at first so Paula accompanied him. Searching for it was the only way to convince Thomas there was no such book at Paula's house. There wasn't much room to search in Paula's small flat. Nothing was found and with only one minute to spare Paula turned and quickly asked, 'Actually, Sidney, how are you? Beverly and I were only talking about you the other day and are wondering if you would like to come over to one of us, maybe, when you have the time.'

'I'm only here because of Thomas.'

'I know, but how are you?'

'You mean after dad's funeral?'

'I mean how you are, full stop. Do you still suffer from what dad did with us? I do and Beverly does.'

'I'm fine on my own, Paula, absolutely fine. I have two dogs and they are great. You will have to come to me, maybe, rather than I you. I don't like meeting people in the streets. I think my ten minutes are up, better go now.'

'Sidney,' Paula said while opening the front door, 'keep in touch. If I don't hear from you in a few days I will come over to see you.'

'That will be good. Bye.'

Sidney ran at top speed back to Thomas's car and with his long legs, stepped inside. Once seated, he strapped himself in and remained silent, wanting Thomas to ask the questions.

'Didn't Paula give it to you?' he asked before turning on the ignition.

'She doesn't have it. She didn't know anything about a book. We searched every nook and cranny, for Beverly's sake but no book was found.'

'Are you sure, Sidney, this is urgent. Beverly wants to read it while she's ill. She won't have time when she's better.'

'I'm positive, there's no book in Paula's house. You can search for it yourself if you don't believe me.'

'That is out of the question, I don't know about the book.'

'But you just told me you knew Paula had it, that Beverly said.'

'Well, maybe Beverly got it wrong, that's all I can say or think.'

Thomas drove Sidney back to the farm in pensive thought. He ended the journey by suggesting to Sidney, 'Beverly doesn't have it, Paula doesn't have it, and Carl doesn't seem to have it. Do you have it somewhere, Sidney?'

'Of course I don't have it. How could I? I know nothing about any journal but I sure wish I could see what my dad wrote in it if there is such a thing.'

'Oh, there is definitely one.' Thomas couldn't help himself. The words tumbled out like a stacked cupboard full of toys when its door was opened.

'Well, I better get back to my pigs,' said Sidney and bade goodbye.

Thomas returned home. Beverly had been unable to rest and so had gone downstairs after a short nap, to wash up. She heard Thomas open the door and called out, 'You've been gone quite some time.'

'Yes, there were queues at the pumps. Had to wait and wait.'

As far as Beverly was concerned it was quite unusual for there to be so much of a hold up at the pumps but for peace' sake she did not argue. She faced another night of tension and what felt like a huge brick wall facing her.

Meanwhile, Sidney lay in bed thinking about his dad. Old memories stirred themselves in a grey blur but one or two sharp memories refocused. He wrote a journal. Beverly has flu. *I will go and see her tomorrow.* The farmer's wife has a recipe for flu. Beverly will be up and running in no time. The following day he would brave himself to the streets. He tried to work out the best time they would be empty. Asking Mr Feathergill after breakfast what time he could go when the streets were relatively empty he made sure he didn't mention any journal, just that Beverly was ill. Mrs Feathergill already had home made concoctions of lemon, honey and ginger stocked for the winter months and handed Sidney a bottle. It would take him about thirty minutes to cycle over there, he surmised. He left straight after lunch. He pressed his feet down on the pedals while tackling the hill then dismounted and, feeling nervous, wheeled his bicycle the rest of the way up the drive. He rang the doorbell and, though the pig smell was far behind him, braced himself for meeting his sister. Thomas answered his knock. Both men stared at each other for some time before Sidney removed the bottle from his jacket pocket. Beverly strolled in from the garden looking quite well. Sidney almost dropped the bottle, declaring, 'Thomas, you said…'

'Yes, I did, I was wrong, it was PMT.'

'Oh.'

'She's better now.'

Thomas stepped to the outside and firmly took Sidney by the shoulder, pulling the door to. 'I, I hadn't expected you to come and see Beverly.'

'She's my sister. Did she say anything about the journal?'

'Don't say anything to Beverly about last night except you heard from me that she had flu. Tell her you brought her some medicine because you were told she had flu.'

Beverly was standing the other side of the door and listened quietly before slipping back to the kitchen. What had he been saying to Sidney? Thomas brought Sidney in. It was no good hiding him or sending him packing, Beverly had seen him and it would be a bad sign.

Beverly wondered why Thomas had not come home early last night. He had gone for petrol had he not? Now she knew he was lying. Sidney handed her the medicine together with the prescribed words from Thomas.

'Sorry, Beverly, Thomas mistook it for PMT. But I'm sure you can keep this.'

'Mistook what for PMT?'

'The flu.'

90

'What flu? I was just tired, Thomas; no flu, no PMT.' Best say nothing more. Ask no questions, get no further lies and save on stress.

Thomas withdrew to the garden. Beverly offered Sidney some tea but he declined politely. He felt awkward being in the midst of some kind of game.

'Before you go Sidney, what did Thomas say to you?' she whispered.

'He told me not to say, but you are my sister. If I start telling you he may come in. It would be better if you came to see me on your own. You can bring Paula if you like.' He left it at that.

Carrying a bunch of carrots Thomas re-emerged. Sidney took note of his stormy expression. He retreated and, turning, walked back down the hall with his hands in his pockets, towards the door. Thomas and Beverly followed. Sidney swiveled his head to face Thomas. The two men stared, neither trusted the other.

'Bye.' Sidney waved and slammed the door behind him. A peaceful life, that's all he asks for. Worn out at such a young age, not outwardly; but inwardly. As he reached the farm, having again braved the Gillingham streets and enjoyed the Kent countryside, he thought about his two sisters. Would they come and see him? Did they really care? Or was it merely because they had laid eyes on him, a formality? They had not said anything at the funeral and why had they both asked how he was?

Chapter Four

Beverly, growing even more puzzled regarding Thomas, drove round to Paula's at the first opportunity. Paula opened the door to her knock and invited her in. 'I'm so pleased you came over, Beverly. I wanted to talk with you about the journal. I know who has it. I mean, who knows about it.'

Beverly's eyes widened as she frowned. Taking a seat on the settee she said, 'My guess is it's Thomas because Sidney said something but I don't know the full story. I don't even know it is Thomas. Sidney cycled over to me, would you believe, with some medicine that Mrs Feathergill had made. She is such a kind lady. He said Thomas told him I had flu then changed his mind and said it was PMT. He then explained he only thought it was flu when Sidney turned up and had appeared okay. I had no idea he had gone to see Sidney, I'm so anxious and disappointed that he has lied to me. What are we to do?'

Heading for the kitchen to make the usual cup of tea, Paula encouraged her sister, 'I know it's Thomas. Sidney came round here yesterday evening too. When I asked who brought him, he told me straight out. You know how faithful Sidney is, how we all are. He said Thomas brought him and that I had a book and you wanted it. I ended up searching the entire flat with him, remembering what you said about not telling anyone. I was so shocked to see Sidney. I could have told him. But when he told me Thomas brought him I knew it was he who knows about it. He thinks I've got it, maybe not now seen as it wasn't found here. And Sidney doesn't know we have it either. Thomas will be confused to say the least.'

'It's a good job it wasn't here, Paula and it's a good job I don't smoke or I'd be heading for dad's demise pretty quickly. I could have so easily given it to you the other day with our contract. We better get round the house right now and rescue it. Thomas may search there again by insisting he wants to go there for some more grief therapy or something. Sidney would have told him you searched here with him.'

Paula whisked her coat from the back of her only armchair, not giving Beverly a chance to finish her tea, 'Come on then. So glad I was on an early today.'

The painful expression on Beverly's face told that the tea was far too hot. Nevertheless, she would not be cheated out of it and took two more gulps. Pain scurried down her chest as she swallowed and followed Paula out of the door. Running down the stairs she waited again for Paula who locked her front door then quickly descended the rest of the stairs to the outer front door where she let Beverly out to start her car and drive off. Paula followed in her own car. Time was short as Beverly needed to be home when Thomas returned from work. They would need to leave about four thirty.

Once inside the house, Beverly said, 'If we tell Thomas you are ill, Paula, and I have to look after you he will be suspicious, having made up the lie about me with flu. He'll think we got the idea from him.

Man, I've only just realized; if Thomas mentioned the journal to Sidney then Sidney knows about it too! You see how slow I am? I also think that Thomas got the idea of illness because I have already told him you may be ill and going to the doctor for a blood check-up. He wanted to know who your doctor is but I told him nothing. I said you are a very private person and tell nobody anything for your own protection. You and I must keep communicating or he will get the upper hand if we tell him two different stories. I said your doctor will phone us if there is something seriously wrong. I will tell him towards the end of the week that he has called and will make up some illness. We can make it a short lived one but where you will need to be cared for, for a bit. I'll have to let my ward know too. You'll have to keep up with your studies as well for the exam.'

Neither of them felt relaxed enough to have a cup of tea this time. They hastily took to the stairs and removed the journal from the library. Beverly turned to the papers on the bed.

Beverly in concerned tones mentioned, 'Thomas has been lying all along. He told me he had done more grieving up here but he must have found that letter.' Swiveling her head she followed Paula as she paced back and forth, 'Paula, can you keep still, you're making me dizzy. How am I going to be able to live with him now? And what would he want with our father's journal?' Feeling despondent she sat down on the bed, pushing the papers further towards the middle.

Paula halted in front of her, 'Maybe he's just nosey? He's obviously the one who opened the letter.'

Beverly gripped one of the pads on the quilt and slid the silky material round and round between her fingers. Narrowing her lips and pressing them down onto each other she paused for thought before saying, 'Well, not necessarily. Maybe he knows someone… no, it must have been him. Who else has been here? Carl, but he didn't open anything, I was with him and he would definitely have said. Thomas is the only one I left alone up here.' She stopped to take a sharp breath in as the realization hit her, 'Yes! He asked me to go and get some biscuits, of course. We'll have to get this house finished. No, we can't act suspicious. If we finish in double quick time he will think something is going on. We have to act innocently. One thing for sure though, Paula, he knows one of us has it. If he hadn't of lied, I would not be thinking something was up but he has so it's time to call his bluff.'

Paula sat beside her sister, taking the weight off her feet, 'He knows there's information in the journal about dad. He actually read the note telling him that he should tell us dad loved us, as it was he who opened it,. He should have told you and the rest of us that there was a journal, up front.'

'He's definitely hiding something. We will find out what it is one way or another.'

'Beverly, I know you don't want to look at this but it's all leading to him being your half brother. Why else act this way?'

Beverly stared into the air for a good minute. Her arms prickled with goose pimples. She felt almost every strand of hair on her head rise to the occasion of that awful realization. 'I tell you what, Paula; I will never kiss him again. I will never touch him again. Him and his riches, I would hate to lose that house but I just may not be able to stay, not now.'

Paula patted her on her forearm, 'We haven't proved it yet, that he's your half brother. It just really looks like it. If we find the proof then is it a crime for that, to marry a half sibling?'

'I don't know but all this makes me shiver. We'll have to find out. It doesn't seem right whichever way you look at it. We really have got our work cut out, haven't we? I tell you what though; didn't I tell you I felt something was bothering him?'

Paula looked around the room as though searching the walls for answers, 'So where do we go from here?' She took hold of her sister's hand, held it tightly and reassured her that she would stay by her side come thick or thin then asked, 'Should we tell, Carl? Then all of us will know there is a journal and yet nobody would know who has it.'

'It will certainly keep everybody guessing. The most important thing is getting to that last page together.' Beverly straightened herself up, 'and we must do it now but what do we say to Thomas? How do we go about it without looking suspect? Your flat has already got the all clear so maybe we can leave it there now. We are going to have to stick with our first plan and you pretend to be ill. I will look after you for a week so we will get time to read it. It probably won't take that long but you will have to fall ill today and I'm going to have to let Thomas know you have fallen ill right in front of me. I'll drive you over to our house in my car and leave you there then pack my stuff and drive you to your flat. I won't be able to live with him, not now.'

Fear rose from nowhere, 'How do I cut down the adrenaline?' She took some deep breaths and stood, then stooped to rescue the journal from the library. Handing it to Paula she gently ordered, 'Put it back into your bag.' She lifted the papers from the eiderdown, opened the door of the locker and put them back inside before swiping the eiderdown from the bed. 'Here, once you're in the back seat put this over you.' The eiderdown hid most of Paula from view. She carried it down the stairs, trying to avoid missing her step. Beverly followed close behind. Paula stepped to the side while Beverly struggled to unlock the door as she carried the rest of their belongings. Once inside the car Beverly turned around to her right to pulled up the small black knob to the rear passenger door. Paula threw the quilt in before getting in, closed the door and picked up the eiderdown to cover herself as she lay down. Beverly passed Paula her bag who withdrew it from sight, concealing it underneath the quilt. On second thought she unzipped the quilt and hid the bag inside, rather than underneath, just in case. Beverly backed out and drove back to Sittingbourne and let herself in. Quickly scribbling him a note that Paula had fallen ill and could not be left alone and had to be kept very quiet, she reassured him that he should not worry as she had called the doctor already and he would be coming round as soon as he finished surgery. Leaving the note in his place in the kitchen she sped upstairs, packed enough things to last at least a week and left. Once Beverly put her suitcase in the boot and had started the ignition, Paula asked, 'What are we going to say to Carl?'

'We'll phone him from your house and tell him exactly the same thing we've told Thomas. Only we won't tell him two stories, like Thomas told Sidney. He'll know the truth eventually.'

As Paula felt every vibration of the car penetrate her body she declared, 'I feel like we are two teenagers running away from home. Thomas will never guess that's exactly what we are doing.'

'No, he won't. We have definitely called his bluff.' Beverly laughed.

Paula laughed, Beverly followed suit, and soon they were in uproarious laughter that tears welled from their eyes, running down their cheeks and onto their clothes. After composing themselves and reaching the flat Beverly switched off the engine one more time and pulled on the hand break. Beverly instructed Paula to act weakly when getting out of the car because they never knew who might be watching. Beverly let Paula out first using all her nursing care experience and, trying to keep laughter from returning, helped Paula down the garden path and sat her on the step in front of the front door. She returned to lock the car doors and retrieve her case from the boot. On return to the step she asked Paula, 'How do we get in?' The sisters stifled even more laughs as Paula revealed where she had hidden her bag. 'Keep your head well done if you are going to laugh, Paula.' With her back hiding the eiderdown from any imagined prying eyes Beverly unzipped the bottom of the eiderdown, 'I don't want to bring the journal out of your bag, just the keys. Where exactly are they?'

'In the front pocket.'

Beverly had no trouble bringing them out, rattling them as she did so. After unlocking the door she helped her sister up who feigned more weakness than Beverly intended. Beverly struggled in lifting Paula to her feet. Paula felt the eiderdown under her feet which prevented her from taking any step forward except to fall into the hall bringing Beverly to a crash landing on top of her. 'We hadn't planned this very well, had we? Quick get in so we can hide ourselves.' Paula tried to crawl forward but the quilt would not budge from where her feet had it firmly pegged. She held the top tightly in her hands. 'Let go of it,' Beverly ordered hysterically. Paula dropped the quilt to the ground before asking Beverly to stand up from trapping her beneath. Finally they cleared themselves from the door and shut it. 'Okay, we can be normal now,' said Beverly who remembered she had left her suitcase on the step, 'Before I reopen the door, get out of sight of the doorway.' She unlocked the door and reaching a hand out dragged her case in. The sisters sat for a while on the bottom step to regain composure before continuing up to the flat. Beverly continued her orders as her imagination fired up even more, 'You better get ready for bed so if there's a knock at the door you are ready to jump in. I'll make some tea.'

Once both events were accomplished and they were ready for any sudden appearance at the door, they sat for the much appreciated cup of tea. Leaving it to cool Beverly phoned Carl. He would not be at home yet but it didn't matter. It was probably easier to speak to Dora anyway. After explaining to Dora about Paula's illness but without the repeating the drama of getting her back to her flat, Dora expressed her sympathy and said she would pass the message on. 'Tell Carl we won't be round to the house until Paula is better; hopefully in a week; then we hope to finish and sign it off from the council.'

'Sure thing,' said Dora, 'thanks for letting us know.'

Beverly replaced the receiver, after saying goodbye, to end the call. As soon as her last mouthful of tea was consumed she carried her suitcase to Paula's spare room where she unpacked her things and neatly put them away. She glanced around the well kept room. She would be comfortable at least so would not be suffering too much away from her usual nesting place. Sleeping in a single bed would be a challenge but no doubt she would get used to it. On her return to the lounge she complimented her sister, 'I love how you have your flat, Paula. It looks pristine. The white bedroom furniture has a crisp feel to it. Pure and bright and I love the pink bed covers. Our purple ones are Thomas's choice. Everything has to be his choice.'

'Has he always lived there?' asked Paula. A sense of personal pride and that she had pleased her elder sister lifted her spirits. Apart from the laughter, compliments of this nature had been rare in both of their lives and certainly they should be more numerous.

'I really don't know. When I moved in after our marriage I simply accepted the place; like it had always been there. Of course, it couldn't have been. The question never occurred to me to ask. I will ask, if I get the nerve to move back in. By the end of the week I should know what to do. I will have calmed down a bit by then and you will know what is on that last page. I can't just tell you. We both need to understand how it got to that point.'

'We can read for an hour or two before supper if you like,' Paula said while removing the journal from her bag and placing it on her glass coffee table.

Beverly reached for it from the settee and opened to the page they had left at.

'I need the toilet first,' she said, putting it back on the table.

Paula leaned forward to search for where Beverly would start reading. For a second she wondered if she had time to flip to the last page but no, she mustn't. She had given her promise so leaned back and waited for Beverly's return.

Paula studied her sister as she marched back into the room. It had been so long since any kind of bonding took place. Happiness was not a common experience for her but this evening, for the first time in her remembrance a sense of belonging soothed her soul. She breathed deeply allowing whatever satisfaction she could muster to seep into her heart. As they sat on the two seater floral sofa Beverly brought the journal closer and held it between them. They fell silent for a while then Beverly cleared her throat and began reading the next entry which happened to be the loose page at the front, 'We were up to where he described us as children. I'll carry on, "I suppose I should write something about 'her'. That night when she was on board ship she was actually dressed as a sailor. What a nerve! To find her way on board like that, to sneak on, knowing we were anchored for a day or two, well, when I had barely gone up the gang plank to fetch my cigarettes there 'her' was, short hair and everything. It wasn't until 'her' came into my cabin behind me that I noticed she was not a male after all. She must have planned her move, must have been watching me. She seemed to know exactly when to strike and it wasn't anybody, it was me she headed for. It was easily eight o'clock and dark so who would notice anything odd about her? I had opened my tin of tobacco and heard the door click closed. I turned and there she was, removing her jacket. I asked what on earth she was doing and tried to get her out but she said if I forced her out she would scream for help. I won't tell the rest except that women are not allowed on deck with sailors. Not allowed on the ship, full stop. I am a decent sailor and maybe that is why she tracked me down. The others sailors, well, some anyway, were too easy. But her threat made me weaken at the knees. To be held accountable for what I did not even trigger off was not welcome at all. I could never live it down. The shame that would have brought on me!

'"When she had won me over and finished why she came she warned me that if I should say anything she would tell the Captain what went on. Then she showed me her photograph, her long dark hair and uniform made her look so attractive. I had actually met her before in the yard; she was a member of the WRNS. She had spoken to me on occasions and I tried to distance myself as I had a girlfriend in Gillingham. I'd known Emma since school days but I developed a soft spot for 'her'. She would tell me stories when she could catch me for a few minutes between jobs I had to do. Even on my way to barracks at various times while ashore she would tell me about her growing up years, how she was parted from her parents. Her parents were rich beyond words. She had everything money could buy. Having things; amazing toys like walky talky dolls, huge teddy bears, small teddy bears, even an undersized penny farthing bicycle and the dresses her mother clothed her in were those fit for a princess. She was an only child spoilt rotten, as rotten as a piece of wood sodden with salt sea for many a year. He told me of how her parents loved to parade her at fetes and parties. Her father had been Captain of the famous ship the Mary Rose, not *the* Mary Rose, mind you, but one she made up to capture my attention. I believed her at the time about that one because of her ability to persuade me of her great importance. I became quite mesmerized as she continued telling her stories over a period of weeks about her entire life.

'"She embellished her story with a tragedy that would make even a statue cry. The day her parents lost it all when the 'famous' Mary Rose sank, leaving her waiting at the quayside with her aunt on a day when she should have been reunited with her father. How her mother had got wind of the tragedy and disappeared from the house shortly after hearing the news, never to be seen again. She and her aunt, in their shock, could only stand and watch their horizon in life disappear. She told me she was brought up with this aunt, who lived alone, and because of her lean way of living she sold all, even the smallest teddy bears and her beloved penny farthing bicycle. Her clothes became rags before too long and all they had to live on when supplies ran out was bread and milk or bread and water and then a mere mouthful.

'"Part of me could identify with her stories because my brothers and I also ate bread and milk, for that is what they were, mere stories, not true at all, but I was convinced at the time that nobody told lies. In my naivety I actually got to like her. If only she could turn back the clock, she said, and get it all back. Not a mention of having her parents back. There seemed to be no bonding there. Only a broken down aunt, whose angry temper was taken out on her, remained. Then I, sad to say, forgot for a while about Emma, when she told me she had been the darling of the sailors.

'"She never lost her love of the sea, never wanted to move away, even from the tragedy. Her parents were out there somewhere, at least the memory of them. Where her mother was she never did find out but as far as she was concerned their souls were bouncing on the ever rolling waves of the sea. At every opportunity she would wait by the quayside for a glimpse of their ghosts but sailors would come along and distract her, moving close and then moving away, mocking her always standing there. Then she said she caught sight of me when she heard about a good fortune I had inherited and suggested how I could help mend her life. How she heard about that is beyond my knowledge and I presume any whiff of a 'rich' scent, carried by an untamed tongue, was bound to reach her ears.

'"I felt her stories drawing me ever closer into her web of lies and deception but I struggled to get away from her demands on me and my money. How do I know the stories were all lies? Sailors told me she was never at the quayside, as she had told stories like it before, until only a week or two before she started telling me the same stories. It was too late by the time I confided in one of them about what she was telling me but that confidence broke when he found out I had been so easily taken in. The seduction of 'her' was so strong. I cannot underestimate the power she had. By then I had fallen for her hook, line and sinker in my heart and she was not about to pull up anchor and sail away. But I didn't recognize her that night with her short hair until under torch light she showed me her photo. She had acted so wickedly but as I remembered her in the photo she was a very well behaved lady, a lady! So I hated her from that night on. I never did find out the truth about her and probably never will.

"'As soon as I had a day's leave after that night, I took off to find Emma. When I found her I asked her to marry me straight away. She was not a double crosser. I didn't see 'her' then for a few weeks as we set out to sea on an exercise. Once we returned I noticed she was right there waiting at the gang plank and I noticed Emma from a distance too trying to make her way through throngs of sailors to meet me. I waved but 'her' noticed where I was looking and who was waving at me and vice versa. I had to focus on both women; one to avoid, the other to greet. The boys were whistling at Emma and making an awful fuss. I needed to rescue her but as I reached the bottom of the gang plank 'her' grabbed my arm. She told me she was having my baby. I almost collapsed. She had to be kidding but she wasn't. Emma was closing in but 'her' whispered in my ear that if I didn't look after her baby when it was born she would tell all and sundry what I had done to her. What I had done to her? Blaming me! I could and would not allow that so I promised her I would take care of the baby. There was no time to discuss the issue as Emma was upon me and I could barely hear 'her' anymore through the din going on all around me. She had the most awful grin on her face and told me she had 'got me in her grip, well and true'. She grabbed my sleeve as I reached towards Emma who was about five arms lengths away and in a loud voice shouted I was never to forget and that she would never let me forget.

"'Finally, Emma made it to me and I clung to her for dear life. As I hugged her I stared at 'her', she was full of jealousy, but held her decency and said nothing to Emma. She simply left with what looked like a smugness I had never known." Oh my word!' exclaimed Beverly, 'I found it so hard not to put the book down so many times. That's the end of another intriguing entry. She sounds like one wicked woman, so deceitful. How awful for dad to have to put up with that. I wonder what happened when the baby was born and I wonder if he ever got away from her and her son. Or if he ever... yes, he will have known his son was Thomas. Maybe her manipulation and blackmail was such that even after if was all over, he could not prevent me from marrying him.'

Paula remained silent as words barely made their way to her mind, let alone her lips. She sat wondering how her father could be silent over such tragic events the way he had. Why had he not divulged all before he died, or even before his own wife died? Surely her mother would have understood? But Paula knew nothing of the kind of sabotage people could play and care nothing for the consequences on others. Finally she managed, 'He had to serve for years though, didn't he so maybe she was there whenever he came home, to taunt him?'

Beverly closed the book after marking the page she had finished at. 'We'll read again tomorrow. Let's have a break. This is really heavy stuff and difficult to digest. It's at times like this, when I would love to go for a long walk but we have to keep up our patient/nurse image so I can't, neither can you. Oh well. Would you like me to cook dinner or, well, you know what you have in your cupboards so maybe you can cook it. I'll help.'

Chapter Five

It was almost five o'clock when Thomas arrived home. He picked up the note immediately on entering the kitchen where he expected to find Beverly. Scratching the back of his head he sat for a while on his usual stool. Paula had been alright when Sidney called round to her, though Beverly had told Thomas that she was not well a couple of days before so he need not be that concerned and Beverly didn't lie. He had not realized how much Beverly really meant to him until now. He thought back to her kiss of yesterday and the time of grief at the house of her father where she had enveloped him. Beverly was precious to him. He had experienced a love of a true family member where his mother had not as much as wished him a hearty farewell on leaving her for boarding school in London. He would have to show his appreciation one day. If only she was not his half sister, he could have had children with her. Before their marriage he had expressly informed her that he was unable to be intimate because of something traumatic that happened to him as a child. She fully understood what that meant so agreed that they could live as man and wife but not that close as to have children. The soft encounters of her touch over the past few days acted to diminish that resolve at times but both of them, in their quiet ways, managed to distance themselves from it, Beverly, both out of her secret wishes and out of respect for his and he, out is knowledge of their true identities. Now they would find out for sure who he really was and that a crime had been committed the minute he put the ring on the third finger of her left hand. His mother, who he had only falsely introduced to other guests at his reception, as a nursing sister from his hospital, made sure they did not abandon the wedding. She witnessed it from beginning to end, until they left for a short honeymoon in Bournemouth. At Ralph's funeral she did not want to be recognized, thus the almost total black covering that she wore, even of her face.

Thomas cooked his meal in silence wondering what he would do without Beverly for an entire week. His job would help use up quite a bit of that time and the gardening and extra jobs there like cleaning the greenhouse and sorting out his tools for the coming spring, would take up more of his time. He thought of nothing more than being reunited with Beverly at the weekend when he leapt to his feet – the journal! He could not allow himself to forget about it. He would call Carl. If it wasn't Beverly, Paula or Sidney who had it then it had to be Carl. He picked up the phone from the counter, sat back down and dialed his number. A familiar female voice answered.

'Hello, is that Dora?'

'Yes, is that Thomas, I recognize your voice. How are you?'

'I'm fine, absolutely fine, thank you. I am ringing to see if Carl is available.'

'He's not home right now.'

'Oh, he isn't home yet but he should be in, in about half an hour shouldn't he?'

'Yes, but then he has his dinner and time with Joseph before putting him to bed.'

'I expect you have heard about Paula becoming ill, Thomas. The doctor is probably with her or maybe a bit later. I'm not sure when his surgery finishes. You can ring Carl, say about seven thirty or eight. Make it eight.'

'So Beverly has told you about Paula then?' he asked, while moving the note around on the counter.

'Oh yes, she always keeps in touch when things like this happen.'

'Ah, okay, well please tell Carl I rang anyway, it was just to let him know I'd had a note from Beverly when I got home from work about Paula. Perhaps he and I could get together for a chat some time. Our times are quite busy but we may be able to squeeze a moment or two in for a bit of socializing. Perhaps he could ring me back tonight and give me a date in the near future?'

'I'm sure; all the best now.'

'Bye.'

Thomas let go of the note and rubbed his hands together. He had saved his skin in the nick of time. Leaping off the stool, excitedly, he caught his foot on the horizontal bar across the bottom of it and landed awkwardly face down on the floor. Pain seared through his leg but he

104

wasn't about to be put off because of that. He tried to get up but could not use his left foot. Turning and rolling up his sock he noticed a slight swelling. Blast, he thought, *where on earth is Beverly now when I need her?* He managed to pull himself up onto the stool again and redialed Carl's number. Dora answered again, 'Hello, this is Thomas again. I'm terribly sorry, Dora, but I just fell awkwardly from my stool and have either sprained or broken my foot. Is there any chance Carl could call round to help?'

'Oh, I, I should phone your doctor if I were you or even the hospital.'

'The surgery is closed and I would never get to a hospital on my own.'

'They would provide an ambulance, wouldn't they?' Thomas quickly thought about that and replied,

'I will call them and get back to you.'

He waited ten minutes then called Dora again,

'Hello, Dora, the hospital first want to know if anybody can take me. Is it possible that Carl could?'

'I'll ask him, hold on.' She mounted the stairs where Carl was changing into his evening clothes. He told her he'd have to give that a priority and leave Joseph for her to sort out. She returned to the receiver in the kitchen.

'Hello Thomas? Carl says he'll be right over.'

'Thank you so much, Dora.' *Well, that worked out okay didn't it? Just when I thought I would not get much time with Carl and I get an entire evening.*

Carl lived the other side of Sittingbourne, two miles beyond Sidney. He wouldn't be long in coming but it would give Thomas time to think about how best to interrogate him. He knew he should not eat or drink anything until they have checked out his foot, in case he needed surgery. He doubted that but to be on the safe side he fasted. Carl arrived quarter of an hour later. Thomas, on hearing his knock, hopped to the front door to let him in.

'Are you alright, mate?' asked Carl, quite concerned. 'How on earth did you do that? Don't tell me, Dora told me, just a formality. Come on let's get you to the casualty department.'

Thomas hobbled on his right foot.

'Wait, have you got your front door key? You can't get back in without it.'

'It's on the breakfast counter. I'll hang on here if you can get it for me.'

Carl retrieved the keys then helped Thomas along to the car. 'Victoria hospital, here we come,' he announced. As he drove out of the drive he told Thomas,

'The last time I was at the Victoria it was too late; too late to see my dying father.'

'And so much has happened since then,' were the only words of comfort Thomas could find.

They had a good half an hour's drive and so Thomas took his time to think about how to quiz Carl. He grimaced in pain from time to time and still could not move his left foot but he had to discipline himself not to agonize too much in front of Carl. He knows only too well what that sounds like. He hears it all the time from his patients at the hospital. 'Do you mind me asking how you got on with your father, Carl? Don't answer if it's too painful.'

'Me? Oh, well, you must know from Beverly how we all got on with him. Has she not told you anything?' Carl asked, while keeping his eyes fixed firmly on the road ahead of him.

'Not much, she doesn't offer much in that way at all.'

'Do you ask?'

'No, I like to think she will offer whatever she wants to.'

'It's good to ask, Thomas, or women don't think you care.'

'Really?'

'Believe me, it's better to ask? You just asked me quite easily.'

'The time never seems right.' Thomas observed Carl's large left hand lower gear as they neared a roundabout. He felt the car slow down and paused to let the traffic pass in front, giving Carl space to concentrate.

'It never will. You just have to ask whenever but maybe not while she's shopping, if you happen to be with her at the time.'

'I just thought you and I could make conversation while we had the time together.'

'I'm okay about it. It's just that sometimes it's better to forget if we can.'

'To get on with your life; you mean?'

'Yes.'

Thomas, knowing Carl could not get out of his presence easily, took opportunity to mention a very important issue, 'I will ask you this, Carl, when you mentioned that piece of paper that you unfolded and read the message your dad had written about, wanting that woman out of his life. Have you ever worked out what that meant?'

'I haven't given it much thought since, too busy with other things; job, son, wife, etc. But it couldn't have been our mother he wanted out of his life as she died of TB. We found her death certificate the next day.'

'Oh, you went to search for that? That was a good idea, to find out for sure.'

'It's what we were told already as to the cause of her death. I just had to go along and find out for certain.'

'Beverly says she had found some letters when you were there.'

'No, I found the letters and she decided they weren't of much use so she will burn them.'

'Burn them? Why? They could become a family heirloom. Burn them?' Thomas fell silent. He became mesmerized with the centre white lines on the road moving backwards and disappearing under the car. He counted at least ten. Carl slowed down at red traffic lights and pulled on the hand break before Thomas snapped out of his solitude. Carl glanced sideways, Thomas had turned quite pale.

'Are you okay? You are very pale, Thomas.'

'It's the pain. Too much pain in my foot, that's all.'

'Here we are,' Carl said, as they turned right into the hospital and parked right outside the accident unit, behind an ambulance. Carl switched off the ignition, walked round to Thomas's side to let him out.

The ambulance man emerged quickly from the doorway, just in time to help Carl get Thomas to a seat in the reception area.

'Why didn't you call an ambulance?'

'I did,' Thomas lied.

'Well, how come you are here by car?'

Thomas ignored the question. Carl waited at reception to give all the details he could about what he knew. The ambulance man returned rather quickly to ask Carl to move his car as he could not get out.

'I'll be right there.' said Carl.

'You really should have phoned for an ambulance,' the receptionist echoed the ambulance man.

'My brother in law said he did. What do I know? He called me to take him so here I am.'

'Well, seen as you're here, you can wait and take him home after he's been seen,' ordered the receptionist.

After the formalities he asked if he could find somewhere to eat as he had missed his dinner on account of this. The receptionist pointed in the direction of a kiosk. Carl found Thomas to tell him where he was off to. 'Sorry mate, I have to eat. I'll buy you something in case it's not too serious and you can have it when you've finished. You must be famished. I'll be right back, save that seat for me, will you?'

'Sure thing. I won't be long, being a consultant. They will see me first.'

Thomas, watching him return to the main doors to park his car in the visitors' car park, envied the freedom of the use of his legs. Growing impatient he let out a loud sigh yet smiled at the patients to his left and right. He had not planned on this at all but one thing he had found out, and a gem at that, was that Beverly wanted to burn the papers and that envelope with their father's instructions would be right there amongst the flames. All evidence turned to ashes. Let her burn it, the sooner the better.

Carl phoned Dora from the phone box before making his way to the kiosk, she answered, the phone beeped for coins. He had little change so had only three minutes to talk. Dora let him know about the conversations she had had with Thomas about the ambulance. When he put the phone down his thoughts braced themselves. He's a liar. His sister's husband and a consultant, trusted by patients with their health issues was no longer trusted by his own brother in law. He would let Thomas talk his heart out but take everything with a pinch of salt from now on. Tomorrow, after work, he would go via Gillingham and pick up the papers. That is one thing Thomas said that could benefit the family and if not him, his son. Beverly made it clear she was not interested in keeping them. It would be a pity to lose them. After eating cheese ploughman sandwiches and enjoying a coffee he returned to where he had left Thomas. Thomas had vanished. He asked a duty nurse of his whereabouts. She pointed in the direction of the cubicles. 'Wait here, Sir, we'll call you when he is ready to come out.' Carl took a seat after glancing at his watch. Thomas's ankle had swollen quite considerably by the time he had reached the hospital. If he had broken his foot who would look after him? Not Carl, not now. He would take him home and leave him to look after himself or maybe drive him straight to Paula's so that Beverly could nurse them both. That wouldn't work, of course, Paula did not have the facilities, or the space, and Beverly had far more on her plate than she could chew. Twenty minutes passed and Thomas eventually emerged, being wheeled in a wheelchair from the x-ray department. He nodded at Carl. Carl waited for instructions from the nurse. 'We're keeping him in overnight for observation. He's torn a ligament quite badly and we may need to operate. I understand also that his wife is not at home right now and is taking care of her sick sister.'

'That's right.'

'Leave him with us then. Our staff get preferential treatment anyway and especially a consultant, as we need to get them up and running as soon as possible. He'll be on the orthopaedic ward at least till tomorrow but he won't be healed for at least six weeks.'

'Okay, be good Thomas,' said Carl, with the emphasis on good, as he waved him off.

Thomas bowed his head somberly before disappearing from view. *Serves you right,* thought Carl as he left for home.

The following evening Carl found the papers back in the locker at his father's house and the bed almost bare. He put them back into the brown envelope and carried them down the stairs and back to his car. Those sisters of his were doing a fine job but didn't seem to have done that much since he was last there. He would give Beverly a couple of days before phoning her at Paula's to give Paula a little time to recover.

Meanwhile the sisters were enjoying getting to know each other better, chatting about many issues on either side. It was Paula's turn to pick up the journal. She read while Beverly looked on, '"Date September 12th 1967, Tuesday. It was Sunday and the war was raging but since the day 'her' came to my cabin I had been unable to function without enormous amounts of guilt and anxiety. I could not trust that 'her' would not tell her version of things even if I kept my side of things. When her baby came I became worried that she would say something to get me into severe trouble. The Royal Navy had far more on their minds than to deal with such an issue anyway, in my opinion.

Emma accepted my proposal of marriage at once as I knew she would but before I could marry her I needed to clear my conscience before God. I had not intended to marry her in such a hurry. I wanted to prepare for it properly but because of 'her' and the rumour of war I thought it better to coax Emma to marry me more or less on the spot.

I was promoted to Petty Officer shortly before 'her' entered my cabin, say about a week, so that made me happy and certainly made Emma happy. Our letters to one another were constant and very sweet. I could not carry on without contact with her and I had served my twelve years contract. If it wasn't for the war I could have left right away if necessary. But the sea was my world and as long as Emma was happy for me I was happy to stay. I was at sea yes in the waters of the earth, but I was also at sea regarding 'her'. I could not concentrate on my work properly and never knew if she would turn up again out of the blue as she had before. Even though I had a clear conscience after visiting the Navy chaplain, the Catholic Priest, and he had been sure God would not hold such a heinous, diabolic act of the perpetrator of my guilt against me, he gave me ten Our Fathers, ten Hail Mary's and five Glory Be's for my penance. I swore to myself never to mention to Emma anything regarding 'her' and her baby would never be part of my life, except that I would have to maintain him from a distance if I did not want 'her' to reveal all. I wrote a cheque to 'her' every time I got paid. It left me very poor and I had to tell Emma I got paid only what I had remaining from what had gone out of my account. Emma trusted me, she never checked up on me. As long as she had me and I her, that was all that mattered.'" Paula closed the book one more time. 'That's the end of that, Beverly.'

'Please read on, Paula, we are getting through and I think we should read all day as fast as possible. I'll read the next two entries.'

'Okay, "'20th October, 1967, Friday. I had only been a Petty Officer for two months and wanted to continue to Chief Petty Officer. Carl was born almost to the date I was promoted. Emma started to write how she missed me because of Carl and that she would love me to be a present father to him. I succumbed to her wishes and handed in my resignation letter. I could not offer any further contract. I had also, because of stress, become quite depressed and unable to carry out my normal duties. I actually became a liability to the Force I worked for and so they accepted my resignation. They could not rely on me in a war situation. It would be too dangerous and put other shipmates' lives at risk. What pay I had received I hardly saw as 'her' made sure her son would be the one to reap my wages. Emma came under a lot of poverty stress as a result and I could not and would not inform her as to why but we managed and eventually Beverly was born and then Sidney and finally Paula. I had got a job as an insurance agent so managed to keep abreast of feeding and clothing our children but mostly, what was left of that after paying, 'her', it was hand me downs for them and the most basic of food.

'"Emma became increasingly weak and sickly and by the time Carl was only eight years old she died of tuberculosis. I did not cry, not even then because fear of being left with 'her' in my life grew to a disproportionate level. Emma was buried in the local Cemetery. I attended her funeral with some friends from the Navy and a few neighbours. The children had to attend as well because I could find nobody to look after them and I did not want to risk them running into 'her' or for anyone who may look after them to be 'her' target. It was, in my opinion, the best for them. At least they were comforted in their grief as I knelt before all of them and wiped away their tears. We hugged for a long time after her coffin was lowered into the ground. I took them every week to pay our respects but I was changing. I had too much to do. The pressure became great and so I laid burdens on the backs of my children. It wasn't just the extra work load that changed me but the extra two people outside of our family. I paid 'her' on the day I received my wages. I couldn't afford a home help. 'Her' said she would come round at times to try to get to know my children but I forbad her. If she was capable of lying to me in such a dastardly way, she was more than capable of contaminating my children. No, Carl became the man of the house, at only eight years old but he quickly grew up. I demanded from him at least a quarter of what Emma used to do. I could not even think of his future. I simply assumed he and my other children would join the Forces as soon as they left school. They would be well cared for that way, just as I had been provided for by them. So, really, I did not worry too much about any careers they might choose. It's all I knew, join the Navy, Army or Air Force.

'"At first my children demanded little but as they grew they needed more and asked for more. It was merely out of necessity but I had nothing to give! 'Her' son had it all! All! And so I started to shout at my children, Emma's children. I became a bear and a wolf to them. Eventually I let go of them, trashed them in my mind. I had to. They were garbage to 'her' and they never saw my smile again. I became a broken, wretched man. I made my children pay for 'her' sins.

'"I wondered if 'her' wanted to marry me so I asked her up front. It was not a proposal. I told her that if she did ever want to marry me she would have to love me and my children, give back all she stole from me and send her son into care. She quickly got the message that I hated her.'"

The phone rang, interrupting the reading. Paula answered.

'Hello, is that Beverly?'

Paula flushed and quickly handed the receiver to Beverly. 'Hello.'

'Hi, it's Carl. I'm sorry to interrupt you being with Paula. How is she?'

'Hello, Carl, Paula is in bed, sleeping. She's so exhausted, it's glandular fever. She has been very sick with a high temperature and won't be up for a few days at the least. This illness can take weeks to recover from.'

'It's a pity she has caught this but I have some news about Thomas.'

'What?' her voice broke and crackled to a high pitch as she spoke. Thinking Thomas had been in touch with Carl about the journal, she tried to stay calm and not blurt out her assumption.'

'Yes, Thomas has severely torn a ligament in his left foot. He's in the hospital overnight.'

'He's in the hospital?' she repeated for Paula to hear. 'How did he do that?'

'He fell awkwardly at home from the breakfast stool. He had just called me on the phone but I wasn't available. He spoke to Dora. After he fell he called back to see if I would take him to the hospital.'

'Carl, he's a consultant. An ambulance would have taken him and even if he wasn't he should have phoned for one, not expected you to do it.'

'It's not really that much of a problem; just put me out of my schedule for a bit. He's in the best hands but, Beverly, we got talking and he mentioned what I said about the letters that were on the bed. You know, those love letters. I told him you said you wanted them burned but he told me I should keep them as family history or something. Anyway, I couldn't trust him. Not after he told Dora that he had called the ambulance when clearly he had not. I've just called round to the house and put all those letters into the envelope. I have them here with me. Just to let you know so you won't be worrying about their whereabouts.'

Beverly lost all colour in her face. The letter about the journal was right inside that envelope. Now if Carl went through those again he would also find out about the journal.

'Beverly, are you still there?'

'Yes, I am, sorry, just had to do something with Paula's covers. They were covering her face.'

Beverly stared at Paula who had not overheard Carl's side of the conversation. Paula mined to Beverly, 'What?'

Beverly shook her head and pointed to the journal but was unable to say anything.

'Beverly, I want to say that Thomas is not who I thought he was when you married him. I respected all medical consultants. I never in my wildest thoughts thought they could ever lie but now I know. You will have to be very careful with him from now on.'

'I know, Carl. Are you sure he tore a ligament or is he play acting? He's not that much of a good actor but I wouldn't put it past him.'

'No, he has definitely torn it. I saw how much it had swollen when he got out of the car at the casualty department. They will look after him, I think, until you are at home to look after him. They know you are caring for Paula.'

'Okay, Carl. About the papers; if you are keeping them I should put them in a safe place if I were you. Like, in the loft in an airtight box. You won't be needing them till Joseph grows up and, even then, only if he wants them.'

'Yes, I reckon you're right. I'll ask Dora to take care of that. I mean to put them in a box as she knows about such things. I will put them in the loft myself. I wouldn't like to risk her going to hospital too.'

'Okay, Carl. Thank you for letting me know about Thomas. I don't know how long I will be here for.'

'You're welcome, Beverly, bye for now.'

'Bye.'

Beverly sat heavily back on the settee and explained what had happened.

'Wow, at least Thomas is out of the house,' said Paula.

The phone rang again.

'You take it this time, Beverly, I better be a bit wiser here.'

'Hello Beverly, this is Thomas. To let you know…'

'I know already, Thomas,' Beverly sighed, Carl just called to tell me.'

'Will you be coming to see me?'

'Thomas, Paula is very sick with glandular fever. She is vomiting nearly all the time and cannot be left.'

'Surely she is a nurse. Can't she handle it? You can return to her after you have visited me.'

'No, Thomas, she may be a nurse but when she is caring for others she is perfectly well. She is not well and cannot care for herself in the same way as she does others.'

114

Thomas continued, 'I don't know how long they will keep me in for. It depends on my foot and it depends on how Paula is. The house is empty as of when I left so I hope it will be alright.'

'It will be fine. Nobody will find it with the lane hiding it. They will take care of you at the hospital. Staff always get preferential treatment, you know that. Please try not to disturb me here. Paula…'

'Yes, I know, Paula needs you badly,' Thomas responded sarcastically.

Beverly sighed again deeply before saying goodbye and putting the phone down.

Paula sat in silence for a few moments then stated, 'You see what trouble I am causing?'

'Paula, you are not sick, remember? This is all planned out by us, except what has happened to Thomas.

'Oh yes, I was beginning to believe all this.'

'I think I might have started to as well. I think it would be safer if we did believe it; that way we wouldn't have to keep finding things to make up.'

'Yes, you're right. Shall we keep reading or wait till tomorrow?' Paula walked over to the window, placed both hands on the glass and watched the twinkle of street lights illuminating the night sky.

'Paula, what are you doing? Come away from there.'

Paula jumped away quickly, 'Sorry, I forgot completely. I was going to draw the curtains.'

'You can't afford to forget,' Beverly stretched up, touched her toes a couple of times then sat back down on the settee. 'It's Carl now I'm worried about and Dora is going to find a box to put all those letters in, so who knows what she will read?'

'We might have to carry on then,' said Paula while pulling the cords tighter on her dressing gown. We will have to tell Carl, if he doesn't find out there's a journal before we finish.'

Beverly stood up to stretch her arms above her head again and yawned. Darkness had long since set a blanket across the green fields opposite the lounge window. No houses or farm buildings faced Paula's flat, which was situated on the first floor of a three bedroom, detached house. Anybody walking their dogs in the fields' public pathways or even the downstairs' neighbours were not trusted at this stage of events. Even though there was little risk of being seen away from the window Beverly closed the curtains, keeping Paula well out of sight. People talk and it's that fly on the wall that knows nothing about anything who spreads dis-ease quite innocently. 'It's late now, let's get some sleep and start again early tomorrow.' That agreed both retired. Beverly lifted the journal from the table and carried it to her room, hiding it in her suitcase. Guarding it was of utmost importance, even from Paula.

Chapter Six

Thomas's night was fraught with worry and pain. With his foot elevated to reduce swelling and his system full of painkillers, he tried to sleep. But sleep would not come. Not without the journal and Beverly. She had been a kind of protection from his mother as his mother did not want to be seen with Thomas at any time. As far as anybody was concerned she was miles away – didn't exist. Thomas never spoke of her, not even under stress. Nobody asked him about her either. It was simply understood that at the wedding his mother was nowhere in the locality, out of sight, out of mind. But that fly on the wall must have been busy. The following morning a familiar figure entered his private side ward. She sneaked over to his side as he was at last fast asleep.

'Thomas,' she shouted roughly in his ear, 'wake up!'

He jumped and squealed in pain. His mother's face peered savagely into his half closed eyes.

'How did you get in here?' he demanded, drunken with sleep.

'Not telling, I'm here to take you home with me. Dora, my niece, has warned me. She was sifting through some papers that Carl brought home.'

'Pardon? Your niece? I had no idea. What papers?'

'The papers from your father's house, she called me when Carl was busy doing something upstairs. He told her he collected them the other night and wants her to put them in a box. He's going to hide them in his loft.'

'But I thought Beverly was going to burn them.'

'No, Carl mentioned to her that you suggested to him to keep them as a family heirloom or something. She knows about a journal your father wrote. She found an opened letter, hidden within the envelope. She read it and told me what it said. You are coming home to me.'

'Why?'

'Well, never mind the reason. It is a reason enough now that you know Dora is my niece. You are my son before you were ever Beverly's husband. You and Dora are my agents, always have been, always will be. Tell me what you know, Thomas. Where is the journal?'

'When you fixed me up with Beverly, did you know she was my half sister?'

'Of course I knew, but now the coals are heating up. Well, your fall is a godsend. Tell me where the journal is.'

Thomas tried to sit up, 'I have no idea, honestly. I'm out looking for it myself. Well, I was. I sent Sidney to Paula's flat and she doesn't have it. Beverly definitely doesn't have it and Carl is oblivious to it. If Dora had not told you about the letter… did she tell you everything that was written in it?'

'Yes. Have you told Beverly that her father loved her?'

'No, I hid it. You know I have to tell you everything first.'

'Well, how come you didn't? Did you open that letter? Dora didn't, she said it was already open. So Beverly and Paula know nothing about the journal, neither of them. I'm wondering that as it is the pair of them who have been sorting out the house… they couldn't have seen that letter or they would have told Carl, surely, and he has said nothing?'

'I… was trying to locate the journal first before I fell. Beverly was resting that evening and I went off to Sidney and took him to Paula's. They both searched high and low and found nothing.'

'Her' helped Thomas up and swung his painful foot off the bed. 'I'm getting you discharged today, right now. You mustn't squeak a word to anyone except that I will be looking after you. Dora won't be saying anything to Carl. She will give all the letters to Carl; he will put them in the loft so I must get hold of that one letter from Dora. Nobody must know about the journal, except us, and we will keep our eyes peeled and our ears wide open. When we find it we must burn it at all costs. The love letters don't matter.'

A young night nurse entered the side ward at that moment to take Thomas's observations before his breakfast.

'I'm taking Thomas home, right now,' his mother announced to the startled nurse.

'But how did you get into the ward?' the nurse asked. 'It's only seven thirty in the morning. Who are you? I'll have to call Sister.'

'I'm Thomas's mother. His mother, do you hear? I have to get to work so how could I come at any other time and never mind how I got in.'

'You are his mother?'

'Yes, now hop to it. I'm discharging him this minute and if you heard anything of our conversation you can forget about it. If I hear that anyone has got wind of anything I shall come back to you and deal with you, understand?'

'Yes, Ma'am,' the pretty little nurse sidled away, letting her out to the nurses' station.

'Her', revealed her name to the Sister in charge as Mrs Worthright, Sadie Worthright. The Sister insisted on her giving her address and phone number so that she could keep in touch with Thomas. Even though Thomas had a pager he was not to use it while his foot was out of action and he must come back for an examination in outpatients in one week's time. Sadie calmed her ferocious spirit down and submitted to all that the Sister instructed. If not, she knew there would be trouble and suspicion. Well, what did the Sister know anyway? But better be on the safe side.

Marching back to Thomas's ward she packed his things and then called the young nurse back by ringing Thomas's bell. The nurse scurried in. 'Get me a wheelchair,' Sadie insisted, 'and then a porter to help me take Thomas to my car.'

'Yes, Ma'am'

Thomas could not believe such a turn of events was possible. He must be dreaming; a nightmare, 'Beverly,' he cried from within himself but nobody heard his cry, no Beverly rushed to his aid. He shook his head. How would he get away from the entire setup his mother had created? His stomach began to churn and rumble in resignation.

'I'm hungry.'

'So am I. We can eat when we get home.'

The porter arrived within five minutes. Pushing the wheelchair ahead of him he found Sadie standing with her hands on her hips, hissing and puffing,

'What kept you young man? All you young people, not snappy enough! Two minutes is all it should have taken. Help me get him into that thing.'

The shocked porter remained silent. His eyes darted from Sadie to Thomas and just as quickly he maneuvered the wheelchair so that no space was left between it and Thomas. He lifted the foot rests so that Thomas could sit down easily.

'Okay, now don't squash the man, or me,' Sadie ordered.

I know what I'm doing; the porter did not show his frustration of the woman. He pulled on the brakes. Addressing Thomas he explained, 'Mr Hopkins, we are taking you to the car. It's pretty cold outside.' He lifted Thomas from underneath his arms and swiveled him as though he was the lightest and smallest of patients. Thomas took hold of the handles and shifted into place. The porter covered him with a hospital blanket then wheeled him to the door of the sideward before turning and addressing Sadie, asked,

'Have you got his belongings?'

'Who do you take me for? What are these?' she held Thomas's bag in front of the porter's face. He did not budge.

The porter thought, *two minutes is what she wanted, two minutes she will get.* He turned the wheelchair so that it faced the exit corridor and put on the fastest pace that left her flagging for breath once they reached the car.

Thomas thought raced just as quickly but he too remained silent. He had met this porter many times and thought what a remarkable young person he was. He seemed to be able to adapt to any out of the ordinary situation that arose, outwitting the most difficult of visitors. Sadie's shocked expression amused both of them. The porter squeezed Thomas's shoulder and both understood the other. The porter nodded at Thomas and after Sadie opened the passenger side door he asked Thomas, 'Are you ready, Sir?'

'Just get on with it!' demanded Sadie, 'Smart alec, that's what you are. I'll report you for your insolence. I could have tripped pretty hard with you running at that speed.'

'That's my usual pace, Ma'am.'

120

The remark had Sadie wondering where he got the wheelchair from in the first place if it took him five whole minutes to arrive with it.

After helping Thomas into his seat and removing his bag from Sadie he placed his belongings on the back seat, swinging them through the gap between Thomas and the side of the car. 'Bye Sir,' he addressed Thomas, 'I hope to see you around the hospital sooner rather than later. Thomas smiled a quarter smile, lifted a hand to thank him but said nothing. The porter slammed the door shut.

'Just be careful with that door,' shouted Sadie, 'I'll have you pay for that.'

'No harm done. Will that be all, Ma'am?'

'Take your wheelchair and push off.'

The porter raised his eyebrows, winked at Sadie, and about turned so as to avoid any further encounter with such a bad tempered old brute. He felt relieved that he was not Thomas and disappeared as quickly as he arrived back to the hospital.

It took only ten minutes to get Thomas home. Sadie lost no time in quickly removing her son from the car. To her he was the product of a worthless sailor so it came easy when the Sister asked her name. Nobody would find her with a name like that. Sadie, that's right. A sailor's right she thought as she struggled to get Thomas in the house. Thomas limped to the fine kitchen. He only lived here during breaks from boarding school. She never made him feel human, like a son. Even though he was thirty two she treated him as she would a good for nothing lout. It was just her, the way she was. He, a medical consultant, the offspring of a female brute, she had no pride in his achievements at all. A tramp, that's all he was. After boarding school it was off to medical school. He was out of sight and that's the way she liked it; left to lap up the luxury that she dragged out of Ralph. Sadie had laughed in Thomas's face as she made him hop smartly from the car to the kitchen. 'Sit here,' she pulled a chair away from the table where he promptly sat in obedience. 'I will feed you but you will pay me. I will board and care for you but you will pay me. You will owe me nothing, you will pay all. As soon as you can walk you will wait on me. We will find the journal and you will never go home until we do.'

'You have a stylish house.' Thomas observed as he was rushed from car to seat. 'Who keeps you?'

'Don't ask questions you will never get an answer for.'

He fell silent and determined not to say another word, ever.

❧

Beverly woke Paula at eight o'clock. Both were washed, dressed and breakfasted by nine. Beverly made her way to her room and gently lifted the journal from her suitcase. 'We better get started right away. We'll read till eleven. When I need a break I'll give it to you. After you've read we'll have a cup of tea and another break.'

'Let's turn the settee round so we can view the fields. I should have thought of that when I moved in but we'll be able to see if anybody is anywhere near the house,' suggested Paula.

'We can't keep looking out of the window as we both have to read at the same time. At least we have witnessed what we have read both together.'

'We can look out at the break, that'll do.'

'Right, where were we? Mum's death and how he hated 'her'. "Dated August 17th 1970, Monday. It's been three years since I started this journal and have only just got to writing more. I am not a well man. All the smoking has taken its toll and has melted my lungs to tar. I have maybe a couple of months to live and that's it.

'"I will say something about how I met Emma. I was frogmarched from that truck I was writing about, with the other boys. The roads and pavements were dirty outside. A tall, awful looking woman met us as the driver dumped us all off. The house was huge with red bricks and small windows with white bars across. It must have been about four in the afternoon. We had been taken to Rochester. The woman shoved us along to a dormitory after ticking our names off on a register. On the beds were a set of clothes and a thin blanket. I could see the castle from my room. The first thing we had to do was make our beds and we couldn't talk to each other. I don't remember much really about those days but first impressions have always stuck with me. Those unhappy years passed slower than I would have liked. I had been there maybe for seven years before I even became aware that there was a girls' orphanage just over the road. I could just about see the castle and

122

cathedral from between that house and some shops. I was twelve when I met Emma. A group of us boys had gone off on our own, like trying to escape in the mid afternoon when the staff were fewer in number. We decided against it because it was so cold outside. It was just before Christmas. Just before we got to our door I noticed a girl about our age sitting on the wall outside the orphanage. She was dressed in nothing but a thin, dirty white dress and moth eaten, pale blue cardigan. She was shivering and crying. I gave the boys the slip and made my way to see why she was crying. She told me a lot of the girls had had visitors and were chosen to spend Christmas with them. So many had left the orphanage and she was outside for just ten minutes to wave them off. She was so sad. I looked into her eyes and despite dirt all over her she had a sparkle of love in them. So soft and warm and yet tears were streaming down her cute little face. Her fringe had been cut crooked and she had naturally wavy, short blonde hair. I sat next to her and we chatted for a while. We agreed on meeting up every day if we could in a secret place that I can't for the life of me remember the name of but it was not far from the castle. We pretended we owned the castle and that it was our home but daren't go in or we would have been nabbed by some lurking policeman. I told her about my brothers and my mother during the time we spent there and she told me about her family. Our tragic stories brought us close together and we were best friends for four years. As soon as I was sixteen I was old enough to leave the orphanage and so applied to the Royal Navy. When I told her she was sad to say the least. She applied to become a maid in one of the grand houses as close to the barracks as she could.

'"While I was at sea we wrote to each other. I had to serve twelve years. I never thought about the amount of time when I applied. If I had I may have changed my mind, to be with her, but where would I have lived? It seemed the best thing. So we became pen pals and remained best friends. When I came ashore she was there every time, never failing. One day a lady came over to me when ashore and she distracted me from Emma. I never realized at the time that she was being forceful but that's what I see 'her' as now. She would pull me aside and talk to me for ages, telling her stories, smiling. Emma was a quiet girl and when she saw this other girl talking to me in her uniform she would politely step to one side. She must have thought she was a Naval authority of some sort. I began to fall for this 'her' as I've already mentioned and so it went on but I never let her get to me in such a way as to defile me. I had been brought up a good Catholic and unless I was to marry I would remain celibate and she knew it. That's why she targeted me. Her mockery that night sucked all decency out of me. I will never be able to live it down, no matter how God may have forgiven me.'" Beverly took a deep breath. 'That's about half way through, Paula. It's very interesting.' She turned the page and carried on,

'"And so it's back to the children. I could not look at Paula as she got older. Her face had formed to the exact shape of Emma's. To distract myself from her as; I would never hurt Emma, ever, I had to ignore her. The hatred I felt for myself had seeped into my very core and my relationship with Paula. I started to hate Paula, especially Paula but I loved her too. I loved all my children and I still love all my children. I am a twisted man. She has destroyed me and my relationships with my own beloved offspring. The ones I planned and wanted. I had to repeatedly tell myself Paula was my daughter and a totally different person from Emma but because Emma was no longer there I put all my 'stuff' on her.

'"One night I lost it with Sidney. He was a real menace at times. He couldn't take orders. Distraction, he was distracted by dogs and other animals and I hit out at him. He's the one who copped whatever Paula may have but Emma was in her and I would never intentionally hurt her. Sidney became my punch bag. I would have nightmares and daymares. The daymares came when I thought of 'her' and Thomas always dogging my steps. I could not kick them off so Sidney got it. Time and again he got the brunt of it all and especially when I came back from paying 'her' her money and if Thomas was there my anger and hatred were dangerously volatile. One day Sidney could take no more and simply went into a trance whenever I came home. One evening he was in that trance but was standing in the middle of the hall and I could not get passed. So I really vent my spleen at him. He felt nothing. At least that's what he portrayed.

'"Only the previous night I had taken the Bible from the shelf in my bedroom and opened it at random. It opened at the Gospel of Matthew. I read the stories of Jesus healing the sick and feeding the hungry. I had said a quick prayer that night for Him to heal my heart and to feed my children. As I punched out at my son I remembered that prayer, especially, 'heal my heart'. It just kind of unexpectedly invaded my emotions like an arrow piercing its victim. I fell to the ground. As I lay there I heard Sidney asking Paula why I hated him so much. I could do nothing but lie still; stiller than still. I never hated him. He was Emma's child. Then as I lay there I realized I was taking out on him the rage I felt towards Thomas. I know I thought Sidney a bit flighty but well, I could excuse myself but if it was not for that woman I would be free to love and appreciate my own children. So I asked God for forgiveness as I lay there and began to sob quietly. I didn't want to draw attention to myself. My tear soaked hand eventually raised me to my feet and later I asked Sidney also to forgive me. How could I look at Paula who was standing across the room, when Emma was right there inside of her witnessing my venom attacking her son? 'Her' venom. 'Her' was attacking my son, through me. Paula would never have understood so I simply didn't try to explain. One day she may understand and if she should ever read this journal, maybe, just maybe, she will forgive me too. So Paula, I address you, that if you ever read this journal, my heart goes out to you, my dearest and youngest daughter, please forgive me for whatever pain I have caused you; a mangled man trying to be a father. Sorting myself out has been impossible but God was surely with me that night as I reached out to Sidney in his room and asked his forgiveness. May God be with us now, even years apart, as I seek to reconcile with you.'"

Paula reached towards Beverly and beckoned her to stop reading. Tears and more tears flowed as she grappled with the reason her father could not love her as he had wanted to. If her mother had not have died… all would have been well. Beverly moved closer to her sister, a lump that had tried to surface in her throat finally arrived and broke into a fountain of tears as Paula wept. Moments passed before Paula revealed, 'I have to forgive him, Beverly, here and now. May God help me. The wounds I have carried all my life thinking he hated every fibre of my being when he was actually loving me and caring that he wouldn't inflict pain on mum, in me.' She broke down again. Beverly reached out putting an arm across her shoulder, as she had to Thomas and enveloped her sister. They cried together for at least ten minutes. They had not looked at the clock. With both of them exhausted Beverly finally released her sister and stood to make her way to the kitchen to make that well earned cup of tea.

Paula waited for Beverly to return, her chest sore from being rent in two, 'We will get over this, Beverly, we will. We will see dad's love for us all.'

'I already see it, Paula, but it's too late. He is dead. I only wish he was right here so we could both hold him, forgive him to his face and live happily ever after but that isn't the case. Life is so cruel.' She handed Paula her mug and a chocolate biscuit to help restore some vitality.

'Thank you,' Paula, slightly shaking hooked her fingers around the huge handle, 'At least we are not dead and can do half of it.'

'Yes, that's something and releasing the pain is so important. This is extra special sister time. There are no hospitals on earth that can heal this pain. Internal injury is by far the most painful and there doesn't seem to be an answer once the tears are shed. I suppose it's the result of letting go of the pain that is the answer. Time will tell how it will be.'

The sisters sat gazing at the fields in silence.

'I wonder, ' started Paula, 'if we will finish the journal today. Can we?'

'I reckon we could if we didn't get so tired reading it.'

'We should try.'

'You can resume the reading after this if you feel up to it.'

'I wish we could go for a walk across those beautiful fields, or go off somewhere for the day to some far off place.'

'Yes, we could always arrange for that some time; after your exams, to celebrate.'

'Okay, let's get to it, can't wait till this is all behind us.' Paula resumed the reading, '"If there truly is life after death, Paula, and if I never get the courage to speak to you face to face I will see you in Heaven for you are sure to be there."' Paula paused from the reading to look at Beverly, 'If there is nothing of value in dad's house, Beverly, I would love to have that Bible.'

'I'll ask Carl for you but only when I see him on my own. I don't want others to be listening. I think I am becoming paranoid,' she laughed.

'Thanks, Paula carried on, "Having said that to Paula and already made my peace with Sidney I want to address Beverly. The same goes for you Beverly, my darling daughter. You are so full of love and warmth, always have been and I sense it would take a couple of bulldozers to break you. I have never shown my love in return for yours. I really have no excuse as I have with Paula. You take after me in looks but maybe that's the reason I could not love you – mere looks. At times it was like I was looking in the mirror and especially if you frowned. I saw the angry me when you did that. When you did, it was usually in response to something I ordered you to do. You are not a sailor but I treated you like one so often. Strictness always caused that look on your face and sailors under my authority, once I was promoted, desperately tried to avoid frowning for fear of being thrown into the sea. I'm sure I caused you to fear a lot but your warmth never ceased to surprise me, though I never let you get close to me. I was inclined to snap at the touch of a button and so I held you at arms length. You will never know how much I loved you and love you still. You are my pride and joy. I ask you too to forgive me for the many times I have mistreated you, thumped you even, thinking about my sailors; raging at you when it was Carl's fault or Sidney's. The years have eaten into you, Beverly, but you have borne it all well and I am a very proud father to have you as my most loving of children. You deserve much better in life and I pray you find it, that God in His mercy will make a way of repairing anything I should not have done to you. Please, I ask that you forgive me too."'

Beverly rested her head on Paula's shoulder. 'It's hard to keep on reading this. I wonder what he will say of, and to, Carl. I forgive him, I have to say that so I know I have. How do I tell dad I loved him too? How do you tell a brick wall or a window in front of you that you love your dad? Or how can I look at you and tell you that I loved him. It would be far better to tell him to his face and maybe I will, in Heaven, with you. There will be no other opportunity.'

'No, but that is something we can both look forward to. He made his peace with God and is making it with us through this journal. This is the most precious thing ever, this journal and if nothing else, we will keep it forever. This shall never be burned. We should only let it go from us when we pass away, whichever of us goes last and not before.'

Beverly lifted her head to look at Paula, 'Do you think God can see us? Right now?'

'I'm pretty sure He can, who knows.'

'So let's see if dad addresses Carl here too.'

'I'll carry on, then we can have a break for lunch.' Paula relayed the book to Beverly Clearing her throat a few times she continued, '"And now to my dearest first born son, Carl, to think that you were born almost to the day that I was promoted to Petty Officer, I say thank you for all you have done in obeying my orders. Without your willingness I would have been a much harsher man. To have a father whose dreams were shattered when his wife died and who had his promotion stripped away almost as soon as he got it. You were a star, the shining North Star always in my heart. When I was at sea or not I loved you. But 'her', who will never come into any good that I wish to bestow on my family, almost stripped your very food and clothing from you. How I detest her but your mother knew how to make things stretch. After all she was born in poverty and was expert at making ends meet. If I have failed you, Carl, and I know I have, I am desperately sorry. My rages after your mother died were astronomical displays of sheer madness, craziness but with four children to care for I tried desperately not to place them in orphanages. My children would be brought up at home with me but they never were, were they? You all would probably have been much better off away from home but I, in my crazy state, kept you here in answer to Emma's wishes, your mother's wishes and never would I let any of you go until you reached sixteen. To you Carl, I say a hearty thank you and to you also I ask forgiveness for what I inflicted on you. I regret all of that bad stuff but I will never regret keeping you out of the orphanage."'

'So there's no message here for Sidney,' observed Paula.

'Doesn't look like it. He already made his peace with him in real life. That must have been an awesome experience. I wish we could have had that.'

'I think it's because God must have broken in that night. I wonder if it was my prayer for God to help him that caused dad to remember what he read only the night before.'

'Possibly, let me get back then, "So I have now addressed all of my children and so, no, wait a minute, I must leave a short message for Sidney or something written for him would be left out. Sidney,"'

'I spoke too soon, didn't I?' Paula stooped a little as she leaned forward to cup her face but straightened up immediately, remembering they must witness every word together.

Beverly nodded before carrying on,

"'... you are by no means my favourite child, all of you are my favourites but you are all so different. Sidney, what happened on that dreadful night I wrote about was such a horrific moment of my life and yet it was the saving of my soul. I had more or less already come to that realization the night before. It had been so late and a depression of such magnitude was upon me. Carrying the load alone, of my own soul and, not seeing any way out, I lay in bed with the light on, propped up, leaning against my pillows. The small bookcase stared back at me from the wall opposite. I could not move, only stare. My eyes shifted a fraction and I found myself reading the title of the book, the 'Holy Bible'. I didn't actually take it in, only stared for a good while until it finally dawned on me what I was actually looking at. I shrugged off an idea of getting out of bed as that would have been too much of an effort so I switched off the light and hid myself under the covers. I closed my eyes, even after staring in the dark for a while, but the title did not disappear from my vision. It held on and on. I was unable to get to sleep as the Bible title grew larger the more I ignored it so finally I tossed the covers off and switched the light back on. Getting out of bed I went over and reached out for that Bible. I opened at the Gospel of Matthew, quite randomly, and read all about the character of Jesus Christ. He was nothing like me. I was a finished off wreck. He healed sick people, cast out demons, and cared for people. For once in my life I wondered if He actually existed anywhere in the world. Was He relevant to my situation? I wasn't sure at all but I had asked Him to show me very clearly. The following night I had to go and pay 'her' for keeping Thomas. Thomas was there and I was filled with hate for the pair of them. But I opened my mouth about Jesus. I actually asked 'her' if she knew anything about Him. I ignored Thomas who pulled the most awful face and she poured out such mockery the like of which I had never heard, "Get that --- name out of my house. Don't you EVER mention that name to me again." She blasted me so much that I came to the conclusion that He did not exist at all. He was just a figment of some incredible imagination. This was not the sign I was looking for and so when I came home after being so terribly put down and then found you standing in my way, that was the straw that broke the camel's back, and the rest of it we all know about. Jesus showed Himself to be real that night and I will never doubt Him again. Since then I have read the Bible from cover to cover. I only wish I had not left it on that bookshelf for all those years. So Sidney I have to thank you for your part in the plan of God that night, albeit, you did not understand what you were doing.'''

'Wow, so dad wondered if Jesus was real?' interrupted Paula.

'I still wonder if He is real,' answered Beverly.

'I think He is, Beverly, He must be after what happened.'

'Could be.'

Beverly lay the book back on the table, 'Shall we have lunch? We can read more later. I think we are three quarters through, we may well finish it in a couple of hours. His writing is quite big. We will get to that last page today then we will have to think about where to go from there.'

'What shall we have?' asked Paula, 'Let's look in the cupboards. I can't wait to find out what's on that page.'

Chapter Seven

Sadie Worthright sat opposite her miserable son after breakfast. He's just a little mummy's boy, never grown up. How could he? She had stuffed him in a plant pot with boundaries he could not escape from. A spindly legged lad, Thomas Weed, the boys nicknamed him at the boarding school. He could not spread out his shoots even to make one single friend. Her name, 'Your Mummy' accompanied every teacher's command and later at medical school she became, 'Your Mother'.

Sadie addressed Weed, 'So, my dearest and only son, Thomas, you are in the midst of a frightful situation and you are the one who will remain in it. If you do not do what I tell you and if you mention anything about Dora being my niece to anybody I will personally end your lucrative career, sell your house and leave you penniless. I always win, do you hear me? Dora has been informing me of every move Carl has made, including taking you to the hospital. How else could I have known about it?'

'I was wondering how,' Thomas mumbled, resting his right wrist on the freshly ironed tablecloth.

'Well, now you know and there's something else you need to know too.'

'Go ahead. I'm listening.'

'I thought I had struck a goldmine when I targeted your father. A top secret rumour had gone around the Naval barracks, and from there across the entire riggings, that he had received a lot of money from a wealthy lost relative. At least that's what a bunch of young sailors told me. Naturally, being gullible and needy I believed them. If everybody believed it so much, then I was sure going to be the first to enjoy his fortunes. Assuming that he knew about it, being the recipient, I quickly shaved my head, donned a sailor's uniform and climbed on board his ship one night. Only when I reached the bottom of the gangway did I hear a handful of sailors saying what a ploy it had been. I daren't look in their direction but their presence gave me the chills as they laughed behind my back. It was too late to turn back, I was already there and any turning around would have revealed I was not who I made myself out to be. They had not realized it was me, on account of my shorn hair. When I got to him I told him about the rumour. He didn't know anything about it, poor man, but I told him that if he uttered a word that I had been to his cabin I would give everyone another rumour. That was the night I conceived you. When you were born I demanded money from him, all he had, or that rumour would catch fire and spread around the Naval world. I would destroy his reputation for ever. You see, you are believing every word I have told you. You will never know the truth about anything I say, except of course, that which you have witnessed for yourself, that I cannot argue with.'

Thomas ran his fingers over a small patch of tablecloth then screwed it into a tiny ridge,

'Thomas! Don't do that!'

He let go and smoothed out what he could of the crease but did not apologize, why should he after all she had done to him? He finished her sentence for her, 'That I was born, I can believe but am I really his son? Can I believe that much?'

'You know there is a journal. Your name is sure to be there and I made sure your father's name was on your birth certificate. Let me show you.' She slid off the wicker chair and mounted the stairs; on her return he saw the proof for himself.

'You might as well keep this. Take it out of my sight. Why do you think I insisted you are called Thomas Springfield? To hide your shame! Only those in authority who demanded a copy of your birth certificate know your real name; Thomas Hopkins but Springfield you are to all and sundry in life and Springfield you will remain.'

She stood to her feet and left the house to go to work, whatever that work was, leaving Thomas to think about her despicable character all day.

৯

Beverly and Paula buried their heads in the journal. Paula prepared to carry on reading.

'You can read it all now, Paula, you might as well finish it.'

'Okay, don't fall asleep. "That habitual liar, 'her', has probably told copious lies about her life but before God Almighty what I write in this journal is the truth. I am a dying man and my time is almost over. With what little strength I have I will record all I know so that whoever finds this journal will be in no doubt as to who she is and what she has done to both me and my children. She has never said sorry, never told me anything good and certainly never changed her mind about my paying for her son. I would have had enough wages to care for my children, if it wasn't for her. I weep when I think of my children and what this has done to them, on the inside. But my own insides have perished, literally. I could have given up smoking long ago but the stress kept me puffing and then Emma passing away. Puff, puff, puff, from her death until my death, I have puffed my way through life. When I found out God was real I still had all the stress in the world to cope with and so didn't change that much; just prayed more than I ever did, that God would protect my children from the worst in me. They really ought to be in asylums by now, surely, but thanks be to Him, they are not and I managed to keep myself out of them too.

'"The years I spent in the Navy were tough years for every seaman, need I elaborate? Thousands upon thousands died in the Second World War. I did not but it has left its scars. The tempestuous sea had us, with bulging eyes, staring overboard more times than I can number. I fought in both wars and protected in both wars; World War Two and my own private war. It was all systems go during the war years but we do not discuss those years in the Navy, being trained to watch our tongues at all times and in all places, you never knew who or where your enemy was.

'"I repeat, what I have written here is true, absolutely, and now I will divulge the name of 'her' and her address and all that she had stolen from me, my wife and my children. What she owns now has been bought in my name. I signed the mortgage deed and have paid since the war years for her to escalate to luxury. I know perfectly well that what I spent on her son was not for her son, ultimately. I discovered she had applied for and won a scholarship for her bright little boy over all the years he attended. Her home belongs to me, yet I have never lived there. It was the place I paid her every month and I could only bewail what my family were missing. 'Her' name is Alice, Alice in Wonderland? You could say so, no, Alice Springfield, her address 71 Congress Road, Maidstone, Kent. That is after he son was born. What she earned at her place of work she spent on herself. All her furniture, of which I have many receipts under lock and key, is mine. Everything she owns is mine, apart from her clothing and food. This is why I have to let my children know I love them. It was better that I pay for all I did than to drag, or let her drag, me and my families' reputations through the dirt.

'"And so, what you are about to read is of my last will and testament. It is not recorded in this book but is bound up in Mr A R Watlingstone, solicitors, of High Street, Chatham, Kent."' Paula swallowed hard then turned to Beverly whose smile could not have been wider. 'You mean. You have kept this to yourself all this time? But how? How on earth did you manage?' She blinked a few times, her left hand fled to her shoulder length hair. She pulled on it gently and numbly sat staring out onto the fields. 'I am stunned, completely.'

'Read on,' was all Beverly could say.

Paula brought herself back from the grass that surely was greener on the other side of her childhood and youth, '"My last will and testament will be conducted after my death, naturally, and my children will never do without again. All that Alice Springfield has stolen will be demanded of her and given to my children – when I'm gone. I knew if we had bought anything in her name my children would have nothing and would never be convinced of my love for them. I outwitted her, the brazen lady, by suggesting she paid for nothing. What of Thomas? I do not know what happened to him but he inherits nothing from me. Let his mother care, if she can.

This journal is the evidence my children need to rid 'her', Alice, once and for all from their lives. She will not be in a position to touch them, having been exposed to the greatest disgrace. The ultimate proof lies with my solicitor, my children cannot fail. She will lose everything, the rug pulled out from underneath her feet, at last – when I'm gone. I have instructed Father O'Reilly regarding my funeral to let it be. It is for Carl to decide what to do with the arrangements. I am to be admitted soon to the hospital. All is taken care of. Father O'Reilly has the details of my solicitor but I haven't told him who the executors are, or is. The solicitor will have to contact the executor/s and they will take it from there. I doubt if Carl will come across this journal until I'm gone, if indeed he ever does. I repeat as I said in the beginning: To whoever finds this journal, please promise me that you will tell my story to the rest of the family; promise to tell them that I love them, I always loved them."' Paula stopped reading. 'Well,' she emphasized, 'I'm speechless!'

Beverley at last relaxed deeper than she had for a very long time, 'Now you see why I said we have to read it together and why I've been guarding it with my life?'

'Yes, I do.'

'So, now we have to wait for the solicitor to contact Carl as I'm pretty sure he will be the one who is contacted first.'

Paula, again fiddling with her hair and slightly breathless with the excitement, advised, 'We don't know and can't assume that, it's only been two weeks since dad died, how long does it take for a will to be probated?'

'Whoever does the executing needs to get a Grant for Probate first. So we need to find out who will be doing this.'

Paula took hold of a stray lock of hair and pulled it taught, 'Do you think Father O'Reilly has remembered? Should we have heard by now?'

'Mind you don't pull your hair out. We will need to go to him and ask if he has remembered. We don't phone. Now that you are well and truly my witness, we need to stick together like glue until the entire thing is dealt with.'

'So now we've finished the journal I can jump out of bed totally well?'

'No, I was thinking about that before I got to sleep last night. I will phone Father O'Reilly after all and ask him to come to see you; to bless you and then we can ask him.'

'Great idea, do I look sick enough though?'

'I'll make sure you do,' laughed Beverly, 'but listen, we still have to guard the journal for dear life. If we lose that a lot of evidence will be lost. I know the will is evidence but this is more and works to get rid of Alice wherever she is.'

'I can keep it here now, nobody will find it,' offered Paula. 'Do we tell Carl yet?'

'I think maybe not. We can let the solicitor do everything and then we can tell Carl about the journal.'

'Yes, but, shouldn't he know now because for one thing he needs to know dad loved us. If we tell him... what if he's the executor, being the eldest? We need to tell him.'

'Maybe we should then, and Sidney. We could invite them here and tell them and demand top secrecy until the will is read.'

Paula grabbed the entire back portion of her hair. Running her hands down it she discovered her neck was slightly moist underneath. 'You know I am pretty nervous, I'm sweating at the back of my neck, must be in shock and not realizing just how much. When will you phone Father O'Reilly?'

'Once we've sorted out where to hide the journal, remember it's your Christmas card list, then I'll phone him.'

'Okay, I'll think of somewhere. Let's have a cup of tea, after that we can walk through the rooms, get some ideas.'

'It's a wonder you have any tea left in the house at this rate.'

Paula left for the kitchen while Beverly stood for some exercise. On Paula's return she continued to exercise. Paula placed the mugs on the coasters. Beverly again sat beside Paula who had become totally absorbed in the green pastures opposite. She jerked when Beverly exclaimed she saw somebody walking down the garden path.

'It's only the neighbour, nothing to fret over.'

'Thank goodness,' replied Beverly, clasping her hand to her chest.

Finishing their tea they both stood and plotted the best spot to hide the journal. The size of it could be a problem but it wasn't long until Paula suggested it could safely be kept in her small bookshelf, just like at their father's house. 'I could put it right there, in broad daylight, people never look at the obvious. If they do come here to have another search they will expect it to be hidden away.'

Beverly nodded, 'You're right but I would feel too vulnerable doing that.'

'We could let Carl and Sidney know now so once they have seen it they might be able to suggest where to keep it; if not here, then somewhere else; Sidney's farm?'

'Not likely, with the Feathergills? We don't know them.'

'What about Carl's loft? And didn't Sidney want us to visit him? We could go to his place with Carl, or let them know separately.'

'Good idea. First I'll phone Father O'Reilly, then Carl when he's sure to be home.'

Beverly picked up Paula's phone. As it was late afternoon Father O'Reilly had finished most of his visiting. She asked if he would come and visit Paula the following day. He said he would be there mid morning and bring Holy Communion with him.

❧

Thomas had sat at the breakfast table unable to think. How had his mother found a way into his ward? Maybe he would never find out. He had not experienced her quite so vicious in the past. She had always been dismissive of him but her true colours had never been so bright. If it was true about a long lost relative having given his father so much money that would explain her affluent lifestyle plus the house he now had the good fortune to live in. Yes, he had a good salary but she gave him the house as a wedding gift to lure him into the trap of clawing it back later. Maybe she was not aware of the type of web she was weaving; she merely started to weave and took it from there.

Nobody likes to be threatened, not even Thomas, bad blooded Thomas. He longed for Beverly but, now caught up in his mother's devices, she would be further out of reach but he would not allow it. He sat bolt upright. Beverly, even if she was not his wife, even if she was merely the half sister that she was, he would still admire her. Her qualities of love and warmth magnetized him. He removed his wedding ring and in anger hurled it across the kitchen and directly into the sink. He moved as much as he could across to the sink, dragging his still swollen foot behind him. 'That's it, down the drain you go!' He turned on the tap and watched his vows disappear. Not an expensive divorce at all. A free man ordained one but good enough for now. His mother would pay for what she had done to her mummy's boy.

The gleaming, smooth white tiles on the kitchen floor helped him move across them easily enough then on out of the kitchen. He had never seen the house properly before as she only allowed him into a bedroom, kitchen and bathroom but not the lounge or the rest of the house. Certainly he had never stepped foot in her precious garden. He never saw the extent of the riches his father gave to his mother. That poor, poor man, living in such a pitiful state; Thomas would see to it that his mother would never get hold of that journal. Now *she* would be caught in *his* web. He limped his way to the lounge, opened the door and stepped inside. What a paradise confronted him! The mahogany display cabinet held priceless Royal Crown Derby; hand painted china plates of all sizes, consisting of twenty four carat gold interspersed with blue and red paint and various paperweights, He quickly opened the bottom cupboards and, as he had done with the Royal Crown Derby, he picked up a plate, turned it over and read the make of the most beautiful and priceless dinner and tea set; 'Royal Doulton, Carlisle'. Opening the centre flap he beheld Waterford cut crystal glasses, decanters and tumblers. Man, she is so rich, he thought. She will pay, not me but not just yet. Bone china figurines graced shelves around the walls. She truly lived in heaven but if so, why was she working?

She had brought him home in a green Austin Morris. Thomas wondered what else was in her garage or just around the corner in some hidden outhouse or garage. He dared to sit on her plush cream leather settee and made himself at home. The huge television in the corner looked like it did not belong to the seventies but some future decade, he daren't touch it. *It must be her pride and joy.* He would befriend her and then drop her right in it. From now on it was all number one, and he was number one. Spending another fifteen minutes basking in her opulence he dreamed of the inheritance she would hand over to him. There didn't seem to be anyone else in her life who would be entitled to it, not if he convinced her how he could benefit her first, somehow. No harm in dreaming. After finding a book to be getting on with from the rack underneath the coffee table and reading the first two chapters he made his slow way back to the kitchen for lunch. He found a huge pork pie in the fridge and settled for that. After lunch he levered himself off the chair and again hopped along the floor using his good leg. Holding onto the banisters at either side he made his way up the red carpeted stairs to his bedroom and dared to enter his mother's. She wouldn't be home for at least three hours, he thought. He did not know what she worked as but his guess was she had a day job finishing in the early evening. The double bed, set in the centre of the room, opposite the door, graced with sky blue silk sheets, pillow cases and eiderdown, greeted him. A solid oak double wardrobe, chest of drawers, bookcase with matching shelves, again graced with figurines, lapped up his gaze. *That poor, poor man,* he thought again, well, she will never make him poor. He would see to that.

જ

Carl picked up the phone to Beverly's ring.

'Hi, Carl?'

'Yes, hello Beverly, how are you? How is Paula?'

'She is recovering but I'm having Father O'Reilly call in the morning to bless her with Holy Water.'

'Sounds a good idea.'

'Carl, I have something to say but it is private, very private. Can you come over here tonight or tomorrow? And can you call in on Sidney and ask him to come with you? Please don't let anyone else know you are coming, not even Dora, just one slip of the tongue and, you never know. It's that important and please don't even talk in your sleep,' she laughed.

'I'll stay awake all night,' he laughed in response.

'That means you will come tomorrow?'

'I'll do my best, straight after work, with Sidney.'

'Sidney will wonder what's hit him.'

'So will I, I think. I'll bring something for Paula.'

Carl surmised it had something to do with Paula's health so changed his mind and not waiting for the following day he braced for the visit. Only telling Dora he would not be long, he drove directly to the farm, rang the bell and asked for Sidney. Mr Feathergill asked Carl in after hearing his rapid and urgent knocking then called for Sidney. Sidney clomped from his bedsit at the top of the house to the hallway where Carl stood waiting. Mr Feathergill returned the way he had come.

'Hello Sidney, haven't seen you for a few weeks. How are you, mate?'

'Hi, Carl, what brings you to this place then?'

'I've had a phone call,' he explained then looked around for any flapping ears but finding none he carried on, 'I've had a phone call from Beverly. She has something very important to say to us. She is with Paula and I'm pretty sure it's because of Paula's health. She has called Father O'Reilly and he's coming tomorrow to bless her with Holy Water.'

Sidney frowned, 'So she really is not well.'

'Ask Mr Feathergill if you can nip out with me for a drink. We must not utter a whisper to anyone about anything, until we know.'

'I'll do that, Carl, just wait here.'

Mr Feathergill acknowledged Sidney's request.

'I'll be right down,' he told Carl, before shooting back up to his bedsit.

After a quick wash and, putting smarter clothes on, he equally braced himself for some not so welcome news. During the short drive neither men spoke. The ringing on the door bell caused both women to shrink away from the window, even though the curtains were drawn.

'Quick, jump into bed, Paula; I'll see who it is.'

Beverly fearfully crept to the downstairs front door. The silhouettes of her brothers were unrecognizable through the deeply frosted glass. She pulled the chain across then opened the door slightly. 'Oh my goodness, you scared the living daylights out of me. I was expecting you tomorrow.'

'I thought we'd better come tonight to see how Paula is.'

'Paula? Oh, yes, she's asleep in bed right now but you can come in as long as you are quiet.'

'No problem, Beverly,' promised Carl.

Beverly led the small procession to the flat where Paula stood as healthy as ever in the middle of the room. Her usual flushed cheeks shocked her brothers.

'What are you doing up, Paula, get back into bed,' ordered Carl, 'you look like you've got a temperature, just look at your face.'

'Well, you scared the living daylights out of us both,' she answered.

'You don't look that ill to me,' observed Sidney. Turning to Carl he asked, 'Have you never seen Paula with red cheeks?'

'Come on, what is this?' Carl queried.

'Sit down both of you, how about some tea before we start?' offered Beverly, 'You didn't say anything to anyone did you?'

'Definitely not.'

Paula left to put the kettle on, smiling as she went.

The rest of the siblings sat and waited for Paula to emerge with the tray of tea. Beverly wondered how best to divulge the amazing news. She gave them time to adjust to seeing Paula healthier than they thought. 'Paula is fine, absolutely fine, always was and always will be. Does anyone know how Thomas is?' she asked, directing her query at Carl.

'No, haven't had a chance to ask; I'm not that bothered about him, quite frankly,'

'No? Well, he is my husband but we've had to do something very important here over the last few days. It involves, where's Paula?' She looked round to see her edging out of the kitchen door with the tray. Paula put it on the table and handed round the mugs. Once sitting and all were taking their first sip, Beverly carried on, 'It involves us all. At least us four, not our spouses necessarily but it will affect them at some point. We have to be careful on this one.

'We're all ears, Beverly, tell us more,' invited Carl. He removed his coat, folded it and left it by the side of the settee, on the floor. Beverly stood to pick it up. 'It's fine just there,' insisted Carl.

Beverly sat back down, 'Okay. I don't quite know where to start; at the beginning or at the end; how about the middle?'

'I'll deal with any of those, Beverly, how about you, Sidney?'

'I'm easy.'

'Alright. We are all in for something big, very big.' Beverly walked over to Paula's bookcase and withdrew the journal. She lifted it so that the front faced her two brothers. Paula sat grinning from ear to ear yearning to see the expressions on both their faces. You may wonder why we haven't finished the house yet. Well, this is why. It's a journal. Dad told me about it just before he died and that is why I said I would sort out the house on my own at first. I didn't know whether to tell you when you all came round that day. I wondered if maybe there was something in it that you shouldn't know. Anyway, to cut a long story short, there is something in it you should know about. You may want to read about it yourselves now. Would you like me to tell you right now what the end is? Paula and I have read it from cover to cover together. You will be greatly surprised but I will warn you, there is something maybe you should not know about which is about that bit of paper you found, Carl, about dad wanting that woman out of his life.'

'That's in the journal is it? This is so... well, please can I see it?'

Beverly handed it to Carl. Sidney kept quiet and peered over Carl's shoulder. Carl flicked through the pages and noted the loose page but said nothing, thinking it was the way the journal was and nothing untoward had happened. Beverly offered no explanation either, to protect her sister. 'I would strongly suggest you read the back page and then go to the front and read about how it got to that. You can't take it from this flat. We have strong reasons as to why not. Carl turned to the back and read the back page which gave the instructions to tell his children their dad loved them.

'He loved us? Dad? How?'

'Either turn to the next to last page or to the beginning, it's your choice.' Beverly's expressionless face gave no clue as to what to choose.

'I'll turn over this page and then, whatever,' He turned to Sidney, 'what do you think, mate?'

'I think he loved us, definitely loved us.'

Carl turned the page and first read aloud about the inheritance. His bottom lip dropped slightly, then wide and then wider still, 'Are you kidding?'

'You must now read from the beginning,' insisted Beverly.

'Oh man, I told Dora I wouldn't be long. Can I give her a ring?'

'What will you say? Be careful, don't let on about it.'

Carl phoned Dora to let her know where he was and that he had been concerned for Paula's health as the priest was coming round in the morning. Paula wanted him to stay longer. He would be back as soon as possible. She accepted the excuse and as long as she knew where Carl was she was happy. Thankfully, Carl had not mentioned Sidney.

'It might take you a few hours to read and you are welcome to stay until you've read enough and then come back tomorrow to finish. The quicker the better all round,' said Beverly.

Carl and Sidney read it quietly and quickly, gobbling up news of the opening of a new era in their lives with great enthusiasm. Beverly interrupted to tell them about Father O'Reilly being in charge in telling the solicitor about Ralph's death and why they invited him to visit Paula. They want to find out if he had remembered to inform the solicitor. Beverly asked Carl if he had heard anything from anyone regarding the will. He denied it and Sidney showed no signs of life in that area either. As Carl read through the hours, interspersed with copious cups of tea, he stopped at various points to comment, 'I'm simply stunned. Dad had a terrible beginning in life. And he has even solved the mystery of who that woman is. Oh my, she had a son called Thomas,' he looked up at Beverly. She nodded. He looked down and then looked up again, 'Beverly, have you already wondered who Thomas is?'

'Indeed I have and I and Paula are not too happy but we have to find out the truth; to find evidence that he is our half brother.'

'That is simply sacrilege,' stated Carl. 'Coming to think about it, he has been acting very strangely hasn't he? We won't need much proof will we?'

'At least he's in hospital and I think it's better to stay away from him as much as possible until we can find out for sure,' Beverly surmised.

Paula interrupting suggested, 'We can see if the local records office has any records of his birth. It wouldn't take much. We know the surname of his mother, Springfield. I doubt if she would have used dad's surname.'

The brothers read the entire journal, finishing about eleven. They discussed with Beverly and Paula where they would start looking for Alice Springfield.

'If Thomas is her son, then he would know wouldn't he? He never has mentioned his mother. Maybe to keep her secret or maybe because he would rather forget the woman,' reasoned Beverly.

'Or maybe even, that he isn't her son,' added Paula.

'There's only one way to find out,' piped up Carl, 'I know Thomas and I have agreed to dislike one another, or at least, I, him, but how about I visit him tomorrow evening in the hospital to apologize for not packing his belongings before we left his house.'

'Maybe buy him some new pyjamas and take them in to make up to him,' suggested Beverly.

'Good idea.'

'Sidney, how are you feeling about all this? You are always so quiet?'

'I'm just taking it all in. I can't work out why we couldn't find the journal when we searched here from cover to cover the other night. How come it's here now?'

'It wasn't here,' answered Paula, 'it was at dad's house. Sidney, you mustn't say a word to anybody, not even the Feathergills, and not even a whisper in public.'

'I won't say a word, I love dad, I won't betray him.'

'We need to find a place to keep the journal safely until at least the will has been executed and we are all on dry land, so to speak,' Beverly said.

'How about giving it to Father O'Reilly tomorrow?' asked Carl.

'Oh no,' Beverly squirmed, 'anybody outside of the family will not respect this goldmine. He would possibly toss the entire thing to the wind after a drink or two and would think nothing of it.'

Sidney listened to everyone's ideas and finally offered to keep it on the farm. He would hide it in his guitar case with his music sheets. No one would dream of looking there. Beverly stated she and Paula would think about it overnight and hide it away from Father O'Reilly and then if that is where they should put it, they or Carl would take it around.

'I did suggest you hide it away from people in your loft, Carl, but would it be safe there?' enquired Paula.

'The only person besides me is Dora and she would never go up to the loft. She is scared of heights.'

Sidney agreed it would be a better idea than his as he quite often played his guitar and it could get spoiled when opening and closing his case, even though he would take great care not to damage it.

'Okay, do we all agree with Carl? It goes to his loft?' Beverly asked. The vote was unanimous. 'So once it's gone and in the loft we forget about it.'

'Wait a minute. I've had an idea,' broke in Paula. 'How about we go to the solicitor and hand it over to him, that way it will be well and truly secured. Not that we don't trust you and your loft, Carl, but at least the will and the journal would be in one place, firmly under lock and key.'

'But you mustn't tell Father O'Reilly,' Sidney wisely and surprisingly uttered, 'nobody must know.'

Paula added, 'Yes, when he comes tomorrow just get the blessing. How will we ask him whether he remembered to tell the solicitor about dad's death?'

'That's a point,' sighed Beverly who had suddenly become very tired, 'we could always ask him… no, we can't. We could get round it this way, that we know dad didn't leave a will because of his poverty but what would…'

'No, hang on,' Carl interjected, 'why not go directly to the solicitor? We know his details, through the journal. Just phone him tomorrow, make an appointment and give it to him, easy.'

'Will there be an extra fee?' asked Paula.

'Not sure, ask him and if he says there will be, we'll chip in together and pay,' answered Carl.

'I'm so glad our heads eventually came up with a workable idea; that's great. So we don't really need Father O'Reilly,' Beverly said.

'No, we don't but we can't cancel as I'm supposed to be really ill,' reminded Paula.

'Okay, we'll let him come so at least he can verify our story about Paula being so unwell if we need his witness,' chuckled Beverly.

Carl picked up his coat from beside the sofa and Sidney, standing to leave, had no such coat. He merely straightened the sleeves of his Aran sweater.

Paula, before saying goodbye, spoke to Sidney, 'I'm so glad you didn't come here smelling of pigs. We wouldn't have been able to concentrate. You must tell us some time, if you want to, what dad said to you that awful night when you were on your own with him.'

'It ended up very well though. Yes, I can tell you another time. You can come to me if you like. I won't be able to remember it all.'

Carl opened the top front door to leave. His three siblings followed. At the door Beverly placed a finger on her lips and nodded to her brothers. They understood. Sidney saluted. Carl smiled.

A fracture in the family bones had begun to heal. After closing the doors behind them Beverly, once back in the flat, strode over to the lounge curtains, opened them a fraction and watched as Carl pulled out and began his journeys home. She sighed in relief, 'Well, that's done now. It wasn't bad at all. Next step Father O'Reilly.'

Paula pulled a quizzical face, 'I'm not looking forward to that.'

'You'll be alright. I'll make sure.'

Paula and Beverly slept soundly once they got there and in the morning Beverly pasted Paula's face with a weak solution of white flour and water. Father O'Reilly promptly rang the doorbell at eleven. Beverly answered with a serious look on her face. It wasn't often she observed Father wearing his black hat and overcoat but his Irish accent helped her relax. Letting him into the room he followed her to Paula's bedside. One look at her and he asked no questions. Her face looked ghastly with dried and cracked white lines all over it. She had forgotten to keep her expression static and Beverly had pasted her face too early. Father O'Reilly knelt by her bedside, opened his small black case and taking out the holy water proclaimed, 'Sweet Saviour Jesus, rescue this child.' Paula, feeling the giggles rise into her chest, fought hard to keep them escaping from her mouth; not a muscle, nor a nerve twitched out of place. 'You need the doctor around pretty soon again,' advised the concerned priest. 'I won't be too long here.' He unscrewed the bottle sharply and sprinkled Holy Water on her before adding, 'I didn't realize just how sick the poor soul is, I'll have to come back tomorrow to perform Extreme Unction.'

Beverly, standing close behind him pressed her lips together as she understood only too well how much Paula was trying to hide. Paula could not see Beverly's attempts to keep a straight face. Her stomach ached with controlling her abdominal muscles from up-surging its emotions. *Hurry up and go away Father O'Reilly*, she thought. She had convinced him well enough that she was not going to recover in the near future.

Turning he assured Beverly, 'She'll be just fine in Heaven.' As he stood to his feet Beverly hung her head before saying,

'Thank you so much, Father O'Reilly.'

.Before he left the room he said, 'I've met a lot of dead people in my life but she is by far the worst. I'll definitely be back tomorrow, first thing, in fact, I'd better come back right away, as soon as I can get hold of my box of oil.'

Paula's eyes widened but she kept quite still until she heard him leave the room and the door slam shut. She waited for her sister to return before telling her, 'I don't fancy going through all that again, please.'

'You may have no choice,' laughed Beverly, 'we have to convince him in case Alice approached him about anything, or ever Thomas.'

'Call him to come tomorrow; my face has cracked worse now through talking.'

'He wouldn't remember where the cracks were, would he?'

Extra cracks widened the dark lines on Paula's forehead as the frown deepened.

'Now you've made it worse. If he doesn't come back today, he'll definitely be back tomorrow.'

'I'll have to keep it on then till he shows up,' Paula resigned.

Beverly's shoulders lifted as she let out a howling laugh, 'It's okay, don't worry, I've talked him out of coming back. I told him it was only glandular fever and you'd be fine in a fortnight.'

'Did he believe you?'

'I'm a nurse, how can he doubt me? I told him you were not dying.' If he knew his own sense of humour he may well have chosen an alternative career.'

'You mean I went through all that for nothing? It would have been better for me to have my normal flushed face. At least I would have looked like I had a temperature.'

'And at least we have his witness that he visited you and that you looked really sick.'

Paula, thought for a moment, 'At least it's over with and we didn't back out earlier. Do you think I'm a good actress?'

'He might have just been going along with us when he saw those cracks, who knows.' laughed Beverly.

Paula leapt from the bed to the bathroom, washed her face and combed her hair, 'Oh to be normal again. I just hope he doesn't have second thoughts and come back today to find me up and dressed.'

'He won't, 'assured Beverly.

❧

After dropping Sidney back at the farm, Carl, being reminded by Sidney, determined to keep everything from Dora. He and Dora were normally open with each other regarding their day to day affairs. He would play this extraordinary card very close to his chest. 'Journal' would be a banned word from his mouth from now on. He would also keep his surprise visit to Thomas to himself and anything else remotely connected to the journal absent from his lips.

He pulled up at one o'clock in the morning. After switching off the car's engine and letting himself in, he made a tasty mug of hot chocolate. Everything appeared as it should, tidy and in order. He sat for the duration of the welcomed hot drink. As he swallowed the heat he sensed the hot trouble he could be in if he accidentally divulged any content of the journal. His lounge, flooded with artificial light, brought memories of the, 'nothing hidden, nothing unsolved' motto Dora had made on their first date evening. He had grown from then on to confide in and trust her. It was not long before he grew to love her and asked her to marry him. She accepted with no hesitation. Father O'Reilly had introduced them to each other after one Sunday morning Mass at the rear of the church. It had been merely a quick, 'do you know each other?' Father had been standing at the back in his usual spot next to the Catholic newspapers. Carl always stopped to buy one. Dora had been standing beside him and making light conversation about the headlines that morning and that is where Father O'Reilly stepped in. He loved performing weddings and baptizing children. This would, if he had anything to do with it, be another wedding with many subsequent baptisms to follow. Carl had never had any reason not to doubt her faithfulness but now the truth was revealed, for his brother and sister's sakes and until the will had been executed, he would hold his peace. Dora would know everything in due course. He swallowed the last dreg, put the mug back in the kitchen and crept up to bed. As he changed he could not help scrutinizing his wife's innocent looking face. *You are in for a huge shock,* he thought, meaning about Thomas being his half brother. He fell asleep, exhausted from the stress. The following morning, being Saturday, two days before Father O'Reilly had visited Paula. Dora left him to wake naturally. She had woken up early and become busy with preparing breakfast for herself and Joseph. Once awake the first thought in Carl's mind was that he would go and see Thomas as soon as visiting hours allowed at seven o'clock that evening.

Having dressed and descended the stairs for his own breakfast he gently approached Dora, 'Dora, my darling, I am going out to visit a friend this evening. He is in a spot of trouble and has asked for my advice.' In keeping as close to the truth as possible he would not be in danger of forgetting what he had said.

She, touched by the encounter, yet feeling disappointed, acknowledged his request. Saturdays were their nights in, come what may, but she had to return his trust and give him no opportunity to doubt her. She had become fond of Carl during their eight years of marriage. His integrity, smartness and gentle mannerisms made her feel secure; better than her aunty coupling her with a tyrant. That first approach had not been difficult. She had been watching him for quite some time and felt nervous should she fail to impress Carl. Father O'Reilly had nothing to do with her aunt's plans. Dora was merely following instructions from Alice but was well aware of the malicious scheme. Alice had taught her well over the years how to hide even the most treacherous of character, not through example, that was impossible but through words; sweet, sweet words. Besides, Dora did not have the treacherous character of her aunty so Alice needed to manipulate very carefully what she wanted to achieve through her niece.

After spending the afternoon playing football with Joseph, Carl promised Dora he would make up to her for lost time. He left the house for the hospital after a supper of rich beef stew and dumplings which had a comfort all of their own. Stopping at the small hospital shop he bought a book and crossword magazine for Thomas to bide his time with and then made his way to the reception desk to enquire what ward Thomas had been admitted to.

'He's on Ward Three,' informed the young man.

Carl strode to Ward Three and asked again of Thomas' whereabouts at the nurse's station.

'He was discharged,' the abrupt nurse told him, 'you say you are his brother-in-law and you have no idea he has been discharged?'

'No, absolutely none, I am a busy man. When did this happen?'

'Yesterday - early in the morning. At seven thirty a woman charged into the hospital and adamantly took over. She wasn't the most pleasant of people, leaving our poor night nurse quite shaken up, and off he went with her, no choice whatsoever, a grown man and one of our hospital consultants at that. She said she was his mother.'

'Did she give her name and address?' Carl hid his shock.

'Sadie Worthright. No address.'

'Sadie Worthright? But that's not...' he stopped himself just in time so as not to divulge the forbidden. For a few seconds he wondered if this should be an exception. No, he had to hold on, at least until he had seen his sisters.

'Not what?'

Ignoring her, Carl stood and, tingling from head to foot, quickly turned back to the shop and insisted on a refund for the good he had bought Thomas. Scooping up the rest of the evening's time he raced round to see Beverly and Paula. Once inside the flat he excitedly, and almost breathlessly, made his sisters aware of the sheer nerve of Alice.

'She's given a false name to the hospital and no address but we have an address, don't we?' Have you given the journal to the solicitor yet? I honestly can't remember it.'

'We haven't yet but we did phone him this morning. He wasn't there, we forgot it was Saturday. He won't be in until Monday.'

'Wow; that was close. It's a good job I went today then, any later and we'd be doomed if you couldn't remember it either. Let's write out the details before we hand it in.'

Paula reached for the journal, slid it from the bookcase, turned the pages carefully and stopped at the page where the address was written. 'Of course, she might have moved so we'll have to be cautious in case somebody else lives there now. Here it is, '17 Congress Road.'

'No matter,' replied Carl, 'we will find out very soon who lives there.'

'How?' asked Beverly.

He scratched his blunted chin, 'We'll have to think of something. I've told Dora I'm visiting a friend in trouble, so we've got a bit of time. I couldn't tell her anything far from the truth or I'd never remember what I said. I'd advise you to do the same if you are questioned. It would be easy to slip up otherwise.'

Paula, pulling on her hair again said, 'We'll all have to watch it but we'll have to act fast or we'll find ourselves in a net we can't escape from,'

Carl continued, 'You all work at the hospital, right?'

'Yes,' Beverly and Paula answered at the same time.

'You could have kept your eyes and ears to the ground if you were working there or maybe think of some way you might be able to find out if Thomas had told anyone anything.' Carl suggested.

Beverly answered, 'We won't be back for some time yet though. They know Paula is ill and I'm looking after her. It's not possible. I could phone and ask friends, I suppose, but then that might put the entire state of affairs in jeopardy. We should bring Sidney up to date. Is there a chance you can call around to him? Oh, and did you ask for a description of the mother? We have no idea what she looks like.'

'No, I didn't even think of it. I'll call back right now to ask.' He picked up the phone and then put it down. 'Don't you think it may be a bit suspicious asking for her description?'

'Not really, you could tell them that Thomas's surname is not Worthright so how could she say she's his mother?' suggested Paula. 'His surname is Springfield. The hospital will then be aware of the false name.'

'Very true,' said Carl who then turned to Beverly, 'Aren't you going to try to find the birth certificate to prove his identity?'

'I'm going to do that tomorrow. No, wait a minute, I can't go, I have to be here but I could phone the records office and ask them to do it. It may cost money but at least nobody will see me going there.'

'Exactly,' murmured Carl, 'and how are you going to give the journal to the solicitor, if you can't be seen out?'

Beverly slumped her shoulders, 'Oh man, there is so much to think about.'

'We have to make sure our steps are well hidden and well ordered,' Paula said.

'We are learning,' stated Beverly.

Carl picked up the phone again, called the hospital and asked for who he had spoken to at the reception. After explaining about the false name he said he was not aware of her description but, 'I could find out right now, please hold on.' He called to the same nurse who happened to be passing by to go on duty and asked what the description of the lady was. A minute later Carl replaced the receiver.

'You wouldn't believe this but the nurse on duty was passing by right then so he was able to ask. She said she was very abrupt in her manner. That she had shoulder length dark hair in a perm, wore silver horn rimmed glasses, light beige foundation on and red lipstick. She had either light blue or grey eyes. There was one conspicuous thing on her face; it looked like a pale pink birth mark just to the jaw line, on the right, near her ear. She was aged between fifty and sixty.'

Beverly snapped her hands to her hips, 'Right, now we have her, you can't grow out a perm in a hurry and, remember, they have no idea we are onto them. I'll ring the records office first thing Monday and ask them to look up Thomas Springfield. They should get it right away. That will be one job done. After we obtain a copy of that we will call the solicitor and get the journal to him straight away.'

'My whole world has been turned upside down,' said Carl before he left for home, stating that he would call on Sidney and update him on the events once the journal had been safely deposited; no point in calling him every five minutes.

❧

The sisters spent Sunday playing card games and generally relaxing and enjoying one another's company. They cooked a delicious Sunday roast between them. While pouring hot gravy over her dinner, Beverly said, 'I can't wait till this is all over, even if we are having bonding time between us. It's the stress of it and not knowing exactly how everything will turn out. That's the thing with being in charge. The responsibility on my shoulders and the worry as to whether you are looking after things okay is constantly gnawing away at me. It could still all go very wrong if the journal is somehow sabotaged, even by the solicitor. We don't know him. And what if that woman and her precious son do something to hijack the entire will?'

Paula dug her fork into a roast potato in deep thought and absentmindedly lifting it whole from the plate twirled it around in mid air. Beverly followed suit. Both potatoes faced each other and suddenly a burst of laughter blurted from the two sisters. Beverly leaned back on her chair, lay her fork and potato down on the plate and laughed until tears filled her eyes. More rolled down her cheeks. Paula watched while shaking with hilarity, her potato remaining in the air. As the tears flowed so Beverly's expression changed to one of deep sorrow which turned into sobs of the deepest grief. Paula lay her fork down and slipped opposite to be beside her sister. The absent bonding that had separated them for so long began to take shape. Compassion for her sister moved Paula immensely. A lump arose in her throat. The sounds coming from Beverly produced a wave of empathy the likes of which Paula had never experienced. 'It's okay, Bev, I'm here and I'll always be here for you. I'm beginning to understand all the turmoil between us, Carl and Sidney. It's a very intense time we are going through. Just let all the stress come out. You'll be able to face tomorrow feeling stronger.'

At that moment the door bell rang. Beverly's wet face lifted towards Paula as she tried to compose herself,

'Thanks,' she whispered and struggled to her feet. 'Who can that be?'

Paula, making her way back from the window announced, 'It's Sidney.'

'Sidney? What?' Beverly shook her head as though to bring herself back to her senses.

Paula said, 'You stay here, I'll let him in.'

Beverly waited, staring at the two dinners which were barely warm now. Taking out her handkerchief she blew her nose, took a few deep breaths and prepared her emotions to greet her brother. As Paula re entered the lounge and then Sidney she turned away in case her face had not yet recovered its normal looks. Paula beckoned Sidney to sit down then asked if he had eaten.

'Oh, am I disturbing you? I had a quick sandwich before I came. You two sit down and eat it up before it gets cold.'

'It's already luke warm,' said Beverly.

'You can heat it up and eat it hot, just put it over a pan of steam. That's what Mrs Feathergill does when Mr Feathergill's late.' Sidney ran a hand through his hair, flicking his fringe out of the way.'

'Why not get that cut?' asked Paula.

'Because I like it.'

Beverly carried the dinners into the kitchen. She washed one of the saucepans that had heated the peas, then withdrew another from the pan cupboard and after filling them with water and lighting the gas, placed the two plates on top of the respective pans, covering them with lids. Feeling worn out and hungry she walked back into the lounge. 'They will take twenty minutes to heat up. Sorry, Sidney, you caught us going through a bit of a crisis.'

'Oh, I'm really sorry. Would you like me to leave?'

'Not at all, you're our brother but what brings you here today?'

'I was thinking at work and in bed last night that I could tell you what dad said to me the night he wrote about, beating me up and that, in the journal about what happened after that. You don't know about his life in the Navy but some things he told me might help you to understand that he was just a normal person before meeting Alice. I told you he did love

154

us. He didn't show it because of her. I know he explained that already in the journal but I want to tell you it's the truth.'

'We know it's the truth,' said Paula, 'because of how he addressed us and about the will and everything.'

Sidney went on to explain, 'I was telling Mr Feathergill about him and he said it might help you two to understand him better, to know him, you know.'

Beverly's eyes darted around the room, hitting the wall, windows and rebounding towards Sidney, 'You've told him? Mr Feathergill? Everything?'

Sidney began to sweat. With his hands clammy, he answered, 'No, no, nothing about the journal and the will, just about dad. He already knows some things that I told him years ago but he knows I was here the other day. I told him because I wanted to ask him if I could come today and tell you things you didn't know about dad. I told him that when Carl came around he had wanted to surprise me, that we were going to visit you.'

'Well, that was quick thinking,' said Paula.

'I'm quite clever really, you know,' he laughed nervously.

'Yes, we know,' Paula patted him on the shoulder as she sat beside him.

Beverly sat opposite them and invited Sidney to begin to tell them while their meals were heating up but first filled a jug with water and brought it with some glasses and placed them on the coffee table in-between them and her, 'Help yourselves, if you want a drink'

'You can start now if you like, Sidney, we're ready,' smiled Beverly.

'Okay. First dad went upstairs to get a photograph from his bedroom. He showed me a group of sailors playing with a bear cub on the ship's deck. He was happy then but missed mum. He told me some funny stories and some scary ones but one funny one I remember though I don't know if he was making it up or not. He said the tallest sailor on the ship told him to tell the captain there was water gushing through the porthole in his cabin. His tobacco and other things were being washed out to sea with the waves flowing in and out. The captain didn't leave his post but told dad that if it was true he would be awarded a medal and if not he would be placed in solitary confinement or court marshaled. He said he didn't know if it was true or not but just relaying a message that the sailor told him. The captain thought for a minute and then shouted for sailors in charge of battle stations to sound the siren and for everyone to get ready to abandon ship. He told me to go to the sailor who had told me and say the captain wanted him. "I did," dad said, and when the sailor came and saluted the captain he ordered him to stand on the starboard and get ready to throw a lifeboat and to face the sea. They guy was shaking, dad said. Then the captain gave the command to stop the sirens. He shouted to the sailor who had got ready to lower the lifeboat 'Stop, don't be such a ….. April Fool." It was April Fool's Day and it taught that sailor a lesson he would never forget. The captain didn't do jokes on April Fool's Day but that one time he gave in to them to teach the whole bunch that they must not joke at sea. Dad didn't get any punishment but was the wiser should anyone try it again. Dad was naïve then, he was only about seventeen.'

'That could have been serious,' acknowledged Paula, 'the guy should have told the captain himself, as it was he got what was coming to him.'

'The thing is dad was only a lad and very obedient to anyone who ordered him to do anything, even if he thought it was wrong so could wind up in a lot of trouble. He was happy in the Navy but one of the scary stories was when he was on board an aircraft carrier.'

'What's one of those?' Paula's eyes widened.

'I asked him that too. He said it was a huge ship that carried lots of planes. Fighter planes usually. They were really powerful but needed to be handled very skillfully. One day a plane missed the runway on coming back and it was hanging over the side of the ship. He went back upstairs to get a photo to show me. The ship had a runway, the whole deck was flat and sailors had the job of making everything run smoothly. It was pretty windy when the propellers were whizzing. He didn't tell me too much about these because he didn't think it was right to and anyway, I can't remember that much of what he said. I can't even imagine one of those. Imagine a ship carrying 100 fighter planes!'

'A hundred? How on earth?' Paula found it hard to imagine that a ship could carry anything but sailors let alone airplanes.

'I don't know but they were real. Those were the stories that dad said were scary but I only half listened because I thought he was making a lot of it up to cheer me up after hitting me so hard. But when I saw the photo I believed him. I couldn't remember a lot of what he had said though so I just kept saying yes to him after he showed me the photo but I do know some sailor's died and pilots.'

Beverly listened intently, 'I can't imagine dad living that kind of life and then meeting up with Alice to spoil his entire life. He sounds like he was a very brave and good natured man.'

'That's what I'm trying to tell you. He was. By the time he had finished telling me I was pretty impressed. No wonder he treated us with all that discipline. He had to take a lot himself.'

After quarter of an hour Beverly stood to check on the dinner. It had warmed right through so she and Paula sat at the table to eat. Sidney remained where he was until they had finished.

'That reminds me', said Sidney after politely sitting until they had left the table. 'I asked dad how they ate their food and he told me it was all powder before taking on board, dehydrated, in other words. He had to eat it or he'd starve and at least it was food-ish, he said but he didn't tell me what he ate except mentioning dried eggs, potatoes and things like that. He was pretty tired that night really. We became best friend after I knew something about him.'

Paula asked, 'What did he say to you just before you left, at the front door? I heard you say, "Aye, aye, Skipper."

'Oh that, it was just that he didn't want anyone to know what he had told me but I have told you now, now that it doesn't matter any more. I better get going or I'll be late back.'

Beverly watched as her brother stood with an air of confidence she had not noticed in him before. He was his father's son, she thought and today he is feeling it, a sense of belonging to a man who had become a true hero in his eyes. As if to read Beverly's mind, Sidney stated, 'I admire dad more than ever now that I've read his journal. We all should be really proud of him.' His eyes moistened but he held back the tears. Forcing a smile he added, 'We need to get him some kind of headstone to honour him, if we can.' Both sisters saw him out to wave him off on his journey back to the farm. They stood for a while after he had disappeared out of sight.

'Okay, coffee,' Beverly said on their return to the flat.

They spent the rest of the day chatting about what Sidney had told them and knowing there could be more to their father than they would ever learn. They left the remainder to their imagination.

Before they prepared for their night's sleep, Beverly said, 'If we had never found that journal we would be the most miserable of people for the rest of our lives. It must be awful for anyone who isn't able to find anything at all about their parents.'

❧

The following morning after breakfast Beverly phoned the records office relaying the details of Thomas, telling them she was his wife and wants to have a copy of the birth certificate. They agreed to search and send it right away when they found it. Beverly did not leave Paula's phone number but phoned back in the afternoon to ask for the results.

'Thank you for phoning back, Mrs Springfield but there is no such name for the year you stated, 1938.'

'No? But there must be. There has to be. I will have to tell him,' she bluffed. 'Maybe he will be in touch with you or at least know why and tell me later?'

She put the phone down. Paula had been listening and asked? 'They can't find it? How come?'

'Let's have a cup of tea and think about that one.'

Paula put the kettle on and, once sitting on the settee in front of their get away fields, they drank one mug full and afterwards, poured a second one.

'I wish I had my shadow,' said Beverly.

'What shadow?'

'At home, the grandfather clock's shadow helps me think.' The very moment she mentioned her shadow she sat bolt upright. 'Aren't we dumb? There is obviously another name he could be registered under; Dad's name, it's a thought. Thomas Hopkins, if so and they find it, he is definitely our half brother.'

Without finishing her second mug Beverly redialed the record office and informed the receptionist of the new name. Late the following morning she phoned for the results. Yes, they had found a name Thomas Hopkins, date of birth, 4th February, 1938.

'That's it, that's his birthday, thank you very much. How soon can you send it?'

'Upon receipt of payment, Ma'am,' replied the deep male voice.

Beverly's thoughts raced. She was reluctant to write and send a cheque for them to post the certificate so offered to pick it up and pay cash the following day. She would not be able to ask anybody the family knew to pick it up so she would dash in the car while, 'Paula was sleeping'. The following day she picked it up as arranged and drove straight back. Nobody would have seen her. She rang the solicitor, explained who she and Paula were and made an appointment. He could see her on Friday at three in the afternoon. Paula would be sleeping again.

'I just thought of something, Beverly. The hospital would have surely known that Alice gave a false name as they know Thomas. He works there. They know jolly well he is Thomas Springfield, even though we have found out differently.'

'Yes, they probably do know but they may have thought she got remarried or something. Another thing is that my surname is Springfield but Thomas is Thomas Hopkins. I am, therefore, married under a false name, kind of. Shouldn't I be Hopkins according to his birth certificate not according to what Alice has been calling Thomas?'

'Wow, it's not going to be good for them at all. That's something else to point out to the solicitor. The hospital are busy as well so might not have troubled themselves, but they might have as well and I doubt they would say much to us or even to Thomas about it.'

Friday leapt in before they knew it had been Thursday. Beverly, armed with both the journal and the certificate, made her way down the stairs and out into the fresh air. She breathed in deeply the autumn crispness, filling her lungs, having been cooped up in that flat for so long. The fresh wind blew her hair this way and that but it always managed to settle to look as sleek as ever. As she drove, her heart missed beats a few times. She had never done anything like this before. She would act as though it was second nature. She pulled into the private car park at the rear of the buildings. The solicitor's office nestled between a newsagent and the library. Her alertness grew in case she caught sight of the woman with a dark, shoulder length perm. Mr A R Watlingstone's name etched on the door beckoned her on his behalf. Her face to the ground she rang the doorbell and grappled with the door handle. In a few seconds a figure appeared behind the closed door. Watching an arm reach towards the handle, she took a deep breath before it opened. The man stood as straight as a ruler, rather like a sergeant major. Beverly stepped backwards before he addressed her politely,

'Ah, you must me Mrs Springfield.' Mr Watlingstone reached out to shake her hand. 'It's a great pleasure to meet you. Do make yourself comfortable,' he invited after leading her up the stairs and showing her into his office. He showed her the usual client's seat and then sat himself down. Pulling his chair as far into the desk as possible, he asked,

'Mrs Springfield, what brings you here?' he smiled so that his moustache almost suffocated his nostrils.

She smiled back whilst trying not to burst with laughter at the sight. His balding head shone with the above light bulb's reflection. She cleared her throat, 'I don't quite know where to start. What I am about to say is in total and utter confidence, Sir, and I must know that I have that assurance.'

'Absolutely, I am a man of strict legal adherence.

Stroking her hair to make sure it was lying straight and tidy she looked him straight in the eyes.

'Actually, I hate to be a little dubious but please may I have a receipt of our time together; what time we started and when we finish.'

'Of course, I always give receipts upon payment and yes, if you so desire, I will include the time too.'

'Thank you. Now,' she bent to pick up her bag and withdrew the journal together with the certificate that lay beside it. You may remember, Sir, not too long ago, a month or so anyway, could be more, that a man named Ralph Hopkins entered your office, or somebody did on his behalf. He had made a will. It is all recorded in this journal. He was my father and father of my brothers Carl and Sidney and sister Paula.'

'Ah, yes, I do remember him. Have you proof of being his daughter?'

'Of course, here,' she handed him her birth certificate Paula had reminded her to take it along just in case he needed it. Paula never ceased to amaze her at times.

'I do remember your father, a lovely man, a very sad man too. Yes, he handed me a will.'

'In the journal it says he instructed Father O'Reilly to let you know upon his death so that you can deal with the will. Here,' she opened the journal and searched before pointing to the spot. Has he notified you yet?'

'I can't say he has, actually.'

'So he forgot, just as I thought he had. Well, you can check with Father, oh no… this journal is top secret and I want to have you store it with the will but since I have now told you about my father's death, it needs to be dealt with straight away but we have found a problem.'

'Which is?' he leaned forward slightly.

'Perhaps you should read this journal and come to your own conclusions. It will save my time. But I realize I will have to pay you for that reading time. It doesn't matter but please do not take up more time than you must. I cannot afford a slow reader. Regarding this birth certificate, it too needs to be held by you and all in the same place as the will. My husband, Mr Thomas Springfield, is married to me. I mean, illegally. This is his birth certificate. As you read the journal you may come to this conclusion yourself. I could not find a Thomas Springfield in the records office. A member of staff carried out the search. It took me a long time to realize that he could have taken the surname Hopkins on the certificate but not in real life, and here it is, dated 4th February, 1938, his birthday. My husband is no other than my half brother and a consultant at the Victoria Hospital, Chatham. I am a nurse and so is my sister, Paula. My brothers and sister have read the journal which my father Ralph Hopkins told me about when I was at his bedside just moments before he passed away. He has a sad story, to say the least and that left us, his children, apart from Thomas, with a very sad upbringing. We were robbed of much and this could be a major crime, not only what Thomas has done in marrying me but also what his mother has done to all of us.'

Mr Watlingstone sat motionless for a few seconds before disclosing, 'Yes, you have all been robbed of a lot. I have read the will. I will read the journal as quickly as I can. Naturally the will could not be executed until the death of your father, which you now inform he has died. You have my condolences.' He lowered and closed his eyes for a second before swallowing. He could not afford to become emotional in front of her.

'Please do nothing until you have read the entire journal.'

He turned away to cough before continuing, 'I will let you know when I have finished the journal and give you my verdict, where we go from there.'

'Thank you, and please, I am very sensitive to letting things out of my sight. But it has to be this way as the journal could be in jeopardy and we would lose a lot of evidence if it was mislaid or even stolen.'

'Be assured, Mrs Springfield, I will not lose your journal or the certificate or the will.'

'How much do I owe you?'

'We will deal with payments upon the finish of the case.'

'That's fine with me, Sir. Thank you.' She stood. He stood. They shook hands. Beverly turned, feeling like a bird ready for flight. She and her family would soar like eagles once this battle was over. He opened the door, led her downstairs and opened the door to let her out. She rounded the corner quickly and drove the half hour journey back to Upchurch. Her father would be well pleased with what she had accomplished with the journal so far. Using Paula's keys and opening the door she sped up the stairs to Paula's flat, shouted a triumphant, 'tea time,' and dropped her bag onto the carpet.

Paula scurried to the kitchen and boiled the kettle,

'What happened?'

'I'm sure I have met him before but can't think where.' She continued to tell Paula all that had gone on between them, then Paula reminded her,

'We must tell Carl now that it is safe in his hands, well, both it and the certificate, so he can go and update Sidney.'

'I'll do that as soon as he gets back from work which should be… Joseph goes to bed… about eight. Father O'Reilly had forgotten, you know, or maybe just hasn't got round to it yet.'

'That woman and boy, well, man, have no idea what is coming to them,' mused Paula.

'No, they certainly do not and I would not like to be in their shoes either.'

'Let's get a takeaway tonight, a Chinese to celebrate,' suggested Paula.

'I hate to celebrate too soon but why not? This step is, at least, a secure one. It's just a matter of days before Mr Watlingstone gets in touch, I should think, unless he has a whole load of cases on his hands.'

Chapter Eight

The last time Ralph laid eyes on his mother, Audrey, and her other sons was the day her husband Bernard died. Bernard had been declared unfit to fight in the First World War due to poor eyesight, though not so poor that he could not see what he was doing. His health rapidly deteriorated shortly after their eighth son was born in 1916. Audrey, being relieved about the fact that his half blind state prevented him from dying in the war, was devastated at his sudden death. She attended to all her boys with a regimented attitude passed on from her own father. Bernard, aged thirty five when he passed away from an acute heart attack, left nothing for her to be able to cope. He worked as a blacksmith and so journeyed quite a bit to sort out horses' shoes. In the cold of winter, 1916, as he was riding down Watling Street his heart suddenly gave out. His horse, unable to offer anything other than neighing, attracted a patrolling policeman. The policeman, reluctant to leave Bernard, sent a straying boy to run for an ambulance. The news of his death reached Audrey about 2 hours later. Attempts to resuscitate Bernard had failed. She was not one given to fear usually but looking around at her eight sons and the youngest being only 3 month old Richard, she knew this brood of young boys were sure to get out of hand. Her husband had rarely been at home anyway so she knew only too well the struggle of looking after them alone. Without an income they were sure to perish, so she notified the State of their plight. The day she took off her apron she vowed never to marry again and regretted bringing her sons into the world. Being a Roman Catholic she went directly to the confessional. The priest absolved her from her duties and left her to say only one Our Father, One Hail Mary and One Glory Be.

Ralph reminded her of her husband in so many ways so she took out her frustrations on him. Nevertheless, hopelessness tinged with remorse of not being able to bring her boys any fortune; watching them follow in their father's footsteps or something of worth and fearing their future she watched as the State, after responding to her cry for help, peeled her sons away from her as rapidly as a plaster being removed from a fresh wound. Her heart bled with each stripping but she daren't show any emotion. Her home empty and her heart sore, she sat in the rocking chair Bernard had made and wept. Five minutes only passed before her crying rose to a crescendo of sobs, the likes of which could have rent the house asunder if it was not fixed securely. She vowed never to trace her sons.

Her head bowed when at Mass, bowed when in the street, bowed when out shopping and never straightened up. A man of her age, a greengrocer by trade, who moved recently into the area, watched out for her keenly day by day. They exchanged good mornings but her returning voice could barely be heard. He asked many of his customers what was wrong and each told the same sorry story of Audrey, the death of her husband and removal of her children. His name was George Haines. He decided to show some care for the woebegone woman and put an extra piece of fruit or a couple of extra potatoes in her bag whenever she shopped. As time went by Audrey's head lifted to snatch a glimmer of his kind face.

'Thank you,' she sheepishly muttered one day on accepting an extra parsnip just before Christmas. Two years had passed since her entire family disappeared. She thought it was a sacrifice for him to donate the goods and it had become a sacrifice for her to receive them but receive them she must, or die. He did not stop giving her extras just because she lifted her head. Her thank you became a smile before too long, to which he returned an equally warm smile.

'You are looking somewhat better these days,' he observed one morning as she walked with graceful steps into his shop. Gracefulness had not been her forte due to her build but for his sake she wanted to put some effort into becoming a little more attractive than he had noted when they first met.

'I'm picking up, thank you, and all because of you showing some compassion and care. And I don't deserve it, believe me,' she chuckled a little. At thirty six years old she felt too old to embark on anything more than banter. She proceeded to buy a bag of mud laced carrots and a cabbage.

'So what will you be eating with those?' George asked.

'Possibly a sausage, one of your cheapest please.'

He reached under the counter and pulled out a large wrapped up pork chop, 'Here,' he offered, 'take it. I salted is especially, so it won't go off for a while.'

'Thank you. You are so kind. I've not met anyone so, well, so, I can't find a single word to describe you,'

'I'm indescribable,' he laughed.

She reached out to take the chop finding it to be extra thick. Looking inside the packet she found there were two, 'but what are these?'

'One for you… and… one for… me?' he blushed slightly.

She hesitated before putting them back on the counter, 'I'm not a good cook, haven't cooked in years.' Her old nature surfaced and she was unable to hide it. All at once ashamed of her inability to cope with another relationship she walked awkwardly to the back of the shop. George waited. She picked up a potato, held it to the light as if trying to see through it, scratched the back of her hand and stared at everything else but without turning her head to meet his eyes should he be watching, "One for you… and… one for… me?" *Alright, but just this once, to thank him for his kindness.* She turned to find him leaning over the counter, resting his arms across the newspapers he wrapped his vegetables in. He was not looking towards her but out of the window onto the street. Passersby swept along the pavement. Many ladies walked alone, others dragged their children awkwardly behind or beside them, all howling. Their husbands and fathers had fallen, killed serving their King and country. Audrey stood to watch for a moment wondering why he had taken an interest in her. But her grief had carried on for many years and no recovery technique had shown any sign of reviving her.

The chops sat just in front of his clasped hands. She walked quietly, yet a little guiltily towards him, picked up the chops silently and tapped him on one hand with her free hand. He turned, his eyes suddenly watering before she said, 'You have been so kind to me that it would be rude not to accept. I will cook in whatever manner I can, as a thank you, just this once.'

George swallowed a whole lot of pain. Not for himself, but for her and the other women he had witnessed outside. It would be so sad if she could not have accepted this chance of broadening her life; it would be such a waste to go downhill again. He would not ask a second time. Not being a man of force he would resign and wait until somebody else in need caught his eye. 'Fine,' is all he could manage.

'I'll have to cook them pretty well straight away as I have nowhere to store them.'

He leaned forward slightly, 'How about this evening then, is that too soon?'

'No, not at all, to thank you would be an honour.' She left for home but turned back to let him know where she lived, 'It would be no good my cooking you this and you not be able to find me.' She left the shop wondering if he really would show up and so allowed her emotions to cool right down. She would not prepare for his coming. If he showed up, fine. If not she would not have wasted her time or energy but she still looked forward in anticipation that his promise would be fulfilled.

At seven o'clock he braced himself against the cold and heavy rain of December 20th, 1919. Securing his ankle length black gabardine, dark blue scarf around his neck and donning his waterproof winter hat he carried a huge bunch of flowers, protected by his umbrella and knocked on her front door, only three streets away. She opened the door expecting to see George in a butcher's apron or similar attire. Her facial expression transformed her entire demeanour at the sight of him dripping raindrops onto her doorstep. He lowered his umbrella, shook it towards the sheeting rain, closed it and leaned it against the wall of her lobby.

'You needn't have gone to so much trouble. Please come in.'

She accepted the flowers, filled a bucket with water and placed them inside.

'I'll help you cook. In fact I will do the cooking,' George insisted, shaking any remained raindrops onto her doormat.

'But, I...'

'No buts, you go and sit down, take the weight off your feet,' he commanded, making his way to her kitchen.

'I'll set my table for us. I can't do nothing.'

George was happy about that and set to cook. She watched as he confidently handled every ingredient. Later when dinner was served

George wanted to know all about Audrey in her own words so asked copious questions. Her neighbours had got it right; no Chinese whispers there, 'So what has become of your children, your sons?' He balanced his knife and fork on the rim of his full plate.

'I totally let go of every one of them. I didn't even keep the date of their birthdays. I am certain they will have done better than if they were being brought up by me but who knows.'

'They may well try to find you one day.'

'I suppose.'

'Would you like to find them?'

At eighty eight years of age she reminisced back to that day. She had pondered the question for the rest of her life. She had been happily married to George for over forty five years. There were no children with George. The two of them had worked happily together saving money for her eight sons. It had not been her idea but his, for her sake. They spent nothing on themselves except the necessary daily items for keeping the business running and for their wedding anniversaries. For those George would take her to special places and always ended with a candlelight meal. George passed away only last year when they were both eighty seven. They often talked about her sons, none of which showed up in her life again. Being alone once more and grieving about George's death, her heart turned towards her sons. Even though they never showed up they were still her sons so who would benefit from their life savings if not them? After all that's who they saved it for. They would have felt betrayed and rejected and may even have forgotten that she existed but George had written his will two years before stating that his wife Audrey would inherit all and even though they agreed never to spend it on themselves he, in unity with her, bequeathed all of her estate to her children upon her death. She did not have to worry about that. George had become such a part of her that all she wanted was to join him in Heaven as soon as possible. George had placed his will into the capable hands of his solicitor who was also the executor. He had also asked him to keep the will until after the death of Audrey to save her changing any of it regarding her eight sons.

The solicitor had traced the sons via the Salvation Army and Ralph's portion, a substantial amount, reached him upon her death. When Alice got wind of it she stripped Ralph of his entire portion and there it was adorning her home. Her house and Thomas's house, which she fathomed as ultimately hers, was bought with that inheritance money. Alice bathed herself in the stolen goods for almost a lifetime. She could sell it all whenever she wished, or so she believed.

Alice, on returning home found Thomas where she left him, at the breakfast table. He had made his way back there just five minutes before she entered the house. *Good timing,* he thought. He had been doing his sums and counted the worth of her entire house. He would surely get it all upon her death. His home was already secure so worrying about a secure future would be a thing of the past and he would be able to give up his career well before retirement age, if his mother died before too long. He could not bear the thought of her living much longer and certainly he would insist that she take him back to his house as soon as possible. If not he would call Carl to pick him up at the weekend. His foot was the problem though. If only he had not been so excited but the clock could not be turned back. He would think of a way around the problem. Standing up to his mother had been unthinkable, but that was exactly what he was doing. Last week everything was fine, this week his world had collapsed. Anything could happen just as quickly before the end of tomorrow. He swallowed his pride as soon as she entered the kitchen.

'I'm going home tomorrow. Carl is taking me, it's all arranged,' he lied.

'Have you spoken to him?'

'Yes, he has your address.'

'I'll take you home myself right now in that case. He's not coming here. Phone him immediately to cancel.'

'How come you don't want him here?'

'Don't you ever ask me questions like that! I'm taking you home.'

She hauled Thomas away, not giving him a chance to reach for the phone.

'You can ring him from your house.'

Thomas grinned behind his mother's back. She fell for it completely. Still he would phone Carl later and let him in on the ploy. Alice picked up his belongings and shot out of the front door, opened the boot, threw the tiny bag in and then marched back for her son. Thomas hobbled as quickly as he could to the passenger seat whose door stood wide open. Alice slammed the door shut, hurried round to the other side and started the engine. Thomas turned his head to the outer window and held back a torrent of laughter.

As soon as Thomas reached home Alice unpacked her car of him and his belongings with great force. Thomas almost tripped again as she lunged at him to extract him from the car. She had no patience to wait for him to get out alone. His trembling was not evident and he had not entirely thought through any consequences of what he had told his mother. Alice about turned, leaving his belongings on the doorstep and him to fend for himself. Before he could turn around she had driven down the drive and was gone. He dragged himself to the guilty breakfast stool, after removing his belongings from the doorstep and, closing the door. He sat on its edge, avoiding any further contact with the horizontal bar and picked up the phone. He had not thought about whether Carl could be in or not. Dora answered. Thomas had no idea as to how to respond to the familiar female voice. If she was Alice's niece it made them cousins. He replaced the receiver without speaking. He would try again and keep replacing the receiver until Carl picked up the phone. After three more times at various intervals Carl did pick up the phone.

'Hello Carl, this is Thomas.'

'Thomas? Where are you? I've just been to the hospital and you're not there.'

'No, I'm at home and in a bit of a fix.'

'Why? What? How?'

'I need to talk to you in private, please come over. Don't tell Dora anything, just come. Don't answer the phone before you leave and don't speak to anybody on your way.'

Why not tell Dora I'm off to see Thomas in a hurry? Carl thought. She knew he was in hospital and now missing but had not mentioned it to Carl.

'Dora! Oh there you are. I'm off to that man again who's in trouble, it's serious, very serious.'

'Okay, please don't be too long. I get a bit worried.'

'I'll be back as soon as I can.'

He hurried down the garden path after pulling the door firmly behind him, revved his engine and sped to Thomas's home. Thomas rubbed his hands together in glee and straightened his uplifted expression before opening the door to Carl. Clearing his throat he beckoned Carl in the closed the door. Carl offered his arm to Thomas to hold on to as they made their way to the lounge. Carl sat with a stolid air. Knowing about the man created a wall of intense opposition and he needed to be on the alert for any trap Thomas may have set for him. At all costs he would divulge nothing.

'So what brings you here, Thomas? I mean, why have you brought me here? How come you are not in the hospital?' he refrained from mentioning his unsuccessful visit.

'I'll come directly to the point, Carl. My mother...'

'Your mother?' Carl interrupted. Who on earth is your mother? I didn't know you even had a mother, well not had one, have one.'

'She's a secret, a huge secret, doesn't want to be made known.'

Carl sat plumb against the back of the settee, 'Do you mean she is some kind of secret agent?'

'No, no, nothing like that. She, she's called Alice Springfield. She messed about with your dad many years ago...'

Carl interrupted again, 'Messed about with my dad, what on earth are you talking about?'

'That's why you found that piece of paper. I knew all along who that paper was talking about. Carl, keep this to yourself but I took off with Beverly to do some grieving in you dad's house and I'm sorry but I went through his papers without Beverly knowing. Carl, you must keep this confidential.'

How much more must Carl keep to himself? *Please God let this thing be over!* He nodded slowly.

Thomas carried on, 'She discharged me from the hospital, just barged in at about seven in the morning and frogmarched me out of there. She drove me to her home in Maidstone. I used to visit during term breaks, coming back from boarding school as a boy but was only allowed in certain rooms then. She left me in the kitchen this morning. Well, last night she demanded I pay for my stay and I simply can't let her get away with any more. I scrutinized her house today and man is she rich.'

'Thomas, slow down, and tell me. This house of hers, where is it?'

'Maidstone.'

'Yes, but where exactly in Maidstone?'

'I can't possibly tell you that, Carl. You would be in grave danger.'

'What makes you think I would be in danger?'

'Her, she is wild, wild, wild. She would have your guts for garters…'

'I'm not planning on visiting the place, just would like to know where it is.'

'Carl, I'm being honest with you because we have to catch her somehow.'

'We? She's your mother, not mine. What do I have to do with it?'

Thomas swallowed, he needed Carl to help him with his plans and so must tell him all, or as much as would allow Carl to help him. If he had blown his plans to befriend his mother he must not blow his chance to cement a friendship with Carl.

'Your father, you may not know this but your father and my mother, well, my mother, what can I say? She is a rogue, a rogue!'

'Is that all?' Carl would not put words he knew about Thomas's mother into his mouth, he must say it all.

'No, look, this is really difficult for me because it could spell lots and lots of trouble?'

'For me? Come on mate, tell me. I'm a grown man.'

'You will keep this to yourself, won't you?'

Carl simply nodded but refused to answer. He ran his right forefinger over the edges of his nails without taking his eyes off Thomas and waited for him to continue.

'Your father is my father, there you are.'

Carl stood up suddenly and paced the room, feigning surprise, 'You are joking of course.' Staring at the grandfather clock he watched the second hand pass over the two and then the three until it reach thirty five seconds past the hour.

'No, I'm not. I'm deadly serious. It is my mother that your father wanted out of his life. Carl, sit down, you are making me more nervous than I am already.'

At least the man is telling the truth, Carl thought. He sat down to listen some more.

'Do you know what this means, Carl? It means we are half brothers, you and I. Can we work together to expose my mother and what she has done?'

'Thomas, this is your mother, your living mother you are talking about, people don't just come against their mothers. You say she is a rogue, but what kind of a rogue is she? Has she committed a crime? If she has then the minute you know of it you must report it to the police or you are aiding and abetting, covering up and you will be liable to be arrested, surely you know that already?'

'I'm not so sure about a crime.'

'Well, then you have just admitted to me that you have committed a crime. Are you not married to my sister?'

'Not any more.'

'What do you mean "not any more"?'

'Not legally any more and we haven't exactly, well, I told Beverly, because I already knew when we married, I told Beverly I was not interested in having any physical relationship with her. I knew, you see. At my mother's this morning I even hurled my ring into the sink.'

Carl's head jolted downwards to scrutinize the look on Thomas's face. 'Her ring? Beverly's ring? She was that worthless to you?'

'No, not her, my mother. I got angry, really angry. Mother made me marry Beverly.'

'What? You mean to tell me, you knew all along that Beverly was related to you? What have you done?'

'Nothing, it was mother and now I have done a self divorce on Beverly.'

'By throwing her ring down your mother's drain?'

'I told you this would all spell a lot of trouble,' Thomas groaned.

Carl took time to think. All this could work for the good of his siblings, his real siblings. 'Yes, you are in quite a bit of trouble, aren't you?'

Thomas hung his head.

'But I can help you, Thomas. I will not divulge a word to anyone else, but out of courtesy and to save you the job, I am going to have to tell Beverly.'

'Quite.'

'You have indulged in your mother's wishes all your life.'

'Not indulged. You don't know how dominating and vicious that woman is.'

Carl bit his bottom lip. He almost blurted out, 'Oh, yes I do,' but thank God for his guardian angel who more than likely set a seal on his mouth.'

'Thomas, you cannot divorce a wife that easily, you must go to court and let them know why you were married or why you can no longer keep that marriage. They have to know and you will need that legal separation from Beverly; to be fair on her and allow her the freedom. She will be totally devastated. Merely throwing a ring down the drain does not legally end a marriage.'

Thomas folded his arms then rubbed his eyes, 'I need Beverly, I need all of you. I need your friendship and support. Please Carl, let her know I don't hate her. She has been so loving towards me and especially since dad died.'

'You and I know we have the same father now, but what of Beverly? She thought your father died around the same time and you didn't even show up at our father's funeral.'

Thomas rubbed his knees then looked towards his injured ankle, 'that's because I had an appointment. I told Beverly it was a meeting but it was important, Carl, I had to go and tell my mother. She had been away.

'You are a spy, Thomas. Informing your mother who…,' he almost slipped up again, 'dominates you so much. You must break free of her as well as Beverly. Go and get yourself a new life elsewhere, Thomas. There are plenty of hospitals around the country for you to do that. Apply to them, I will vouch for you if you need a reference, oh no, I probably won't be able to, being your half brother but we could always try.'

'But something has to be done about my mother, I need your help.'

'If you can convince a judge that you had no part in marrying Beverly, except under the duress of your mother, then you might stand a chance of getting away without a criminal record. What else do you know about your mother?'

'There's nothing else, Carl,' he paused, 'except there's a will, oh, I'm going to have to come completely clean here so please bear with me.' Thomas felt he was too deeply entrenched in some ever circling whirlpool and the only way out was to tell Carl absolutely everything or he would not lend a helping hand to pull him out. What if he already knew? If he did he was too damned clever and if he didn't he would find out and that would spell even more trouble, 'Okay, there is, there is a journal somewhere, I read about it… while I was with Beverly at our dad's house. I have no idea where it is but I know it exists and my mother knows it exists too because I told her, before I really knew how so awful she is.'

'Your mother knew…' Carl almost slipped again and refrained from saying, "about the journal?" What journal is this, Thomas?'

'I read about it in a letter dad had written. A note, he wants you all, that is, not me, to know he loved you, that he always loved you. That journal has lots of information in it, the note says, and my mother wants it. She wants me to get it for her.' He said opening a way out for himself. Carl was sure to help him now that he had placed all the blame on his mother's shoulders.

'Wants you to get it for her?'

'Yes.'

'Why haven't you told us all this before now? Why can't she get it for herself?'

Anger, not usually one of his traits, pulsed from Thomas's belly as the pressure increased. Was Carl never going to give in? He sighed with exasperation and waited for words to come but they tarried. He would try once more, 'so you know where it is then; for her to get it?'

The question was too obvious. Carl's words were not late, 'I have no idea about any journal. You are the one talking about a journal, not me.'

'Did your mother say anything else? If we are to cooperate with each other I need to know all she said.'

Thomas looked him straight in the eye and shouted, 'No!'

'Why are you getting upset then?'

'Frustrated is the word.'

'Frustrated then, okay, I will take you back to the hospital so they can keep an eye on you.'

'But what if my mother gets wind that I'm there again? She'll be over like a flash to torment me and even...'

'Your mother won't get wind of anything; I only tell Dora what I do. It will be quite safe with her. She tells no one.'

Thomas raced his right hand across his chest and held his breast bone, squeezing his jumper at the same time. Tension mounted. He was trapped. Opening his mouth he began, 'Dora, tells nobody anything? Are you sure? You can't know her very well then, Carl!'

Carl's penetrating gaze pierced Thomas to the core, 'Of course I can trust her. She's my wife!'

'I'd rather stay at home then, thank you. Please don't utter a word to Dora.'

'Why on earth not?'

Thomas shook from head to foot. He felt like an agitated caged bear. There was no way out at all, 'Because she is my mother's niece, that's why not!'

'You what? You what?' his palms became sweaty, his skin crept, 'are you telling me the truth?'

176

'I am, that's what my mother told me this very morning and people tell the truth when they are livid. Dora and I are cousins. I am just as surprised as you are.'

Carl did not know what to say or do next. He sat on the edge of the settee rocking back and forth. He thought about Joseph, then Beverly and Paula with the journal safely under lock and key. At least it was well out of harms way. He thought of Sidney relatively problem free and envied him his lack of involvement. Here he was sitting beside Thomas who had lied to his half sister and half brothers and whatever else he had done. Now it was Dora. Never in a million years would he have thought Dora could possibly betray him, 'Your mother knows who I am, knows my wife and my son?'

'Indeed she does, Carl.'

'Everything about us?'

'Yes.'

'Man, o man! Well, it's a darn good job I didn't tell Dora I was coming to see you then. That's all I can say.'

'You didn't?'

'No, I said I was going to see a man who was in trouble, severe trouble. She wouldn't guess.'

'My mother is out to destroy you all. She got me to marry Beverly and was responsible for Dora marrying you. She knows all about you, all of you, every step. I'm sorry, Carl, but I've been guilty of telling her, until now, I vow never to tell her another word.'

Carl fell silent, doubly silent, then asked permission to make a cup of tea. The grandfather clock struck nine, 'I need more than a cup of tea right now,' he said as he left the room. Once in the kitchen he picked up the kettle. The water inside splashed up the sides as he shook. The spout was hard to steer as he turned on the tap. As he leaned against the sink, letting out a most forlorn sigh, he heard the faintness of a laugh coming from the lounge, a mocking laugh. He stopped shaking, stood erect and plugged the kettle in. Right, Thomas, old boy, you have it, he shouted silently, within. 'How do you have your tea, Thomas? I can't remember.' Without waiting for a reply and after the tea was brewed he dollopped four teaspoonfuls of sugar into Thomas's mug and refused to stir it. He marched angrily into the lounge carrying a mug in each hand

and stated, 'As soon as I've had this I'm going directly home and am going to come straight to the point with Dora about what you have told me. When she knows I know I doubt she will stay much longer. In fact, I may throw her out! I have bided my time long enough with this issue and now all comes clean. What is your mother's address?'

'No, you can't go to her, Carl, that's why she dumped me back here. She doesn't want you there. I told her I was going to contact you and ask you to bring me back home. She let off a mighty fuse.'

'Well, she may well have to lump it.' He swallowed the final dreg then sucked on it as though he would get another mouthful through the bottom of the mug. 'Take care of yourself, Thomas. You're on your own, mate.' Grabbing his coat he fled the house, slamming all doors behind him. Turning the key in the ignition by an attempted three hundred and sixty degrees he fired up his engine. Smoke rose from his wheels as he screeched to third gear in less than three seconds. He fled to Beverly and Paula. His frantic knocking came just as they were about to fall asleep. Beverly crept out of bed and, keeping all lights off, pulled the corner of the lounge curtain up a fraction. Again Carl knocked frantically. Paula fearfully grabbed her covers tightly over her head.

'It's Carl,' Beverly whispered.

As Paula peered out from the covers with one eye Beverly hurried down the stairs to let him in.

'What on earth has happened,' she enquired as soon as she opened the door, 'Why are you here at this time of night?'

He ushered her, almost pushing her ahead of him. 'Quickly, let's get into the flat.' Closing the door behind him he followed her upstairs. Beverly pushed the door to the flat wider and once they were both inside Carl closed the door. As he passed Paula's bedroom he chuckled at the sight of her still under the covers. She reluctantly pushed away the covers and stepped out of bed, put on her dressing gown and made her way into the lounge where Carl started, 'Okay, let me calm down first. I have tons to tell you. I'm finished with Thomas. Beverly, you are finished with him too and, and, I am finished with Dora.'

'Dora? What has she done?' Beverly asked, astonished.

Paula had woken up properly at that statement, 'Dora?'

'Yes, Dora. It's all a great set up. We have all been targets of Thomas's mother to this day! The first four letters of mother is moth right? She has definitely eaten holes out of the fabric of our family and we need to get together and sort this out, if possible this very night.'

'Okay, breathe deeply as few times, Carl.' Beverly advised smoothly. 'I'm making a cup of tea.'

Paula sat beside Carl, taking his hands in hers.

'What is it? Has he found out about the journal? Have you told him about it? He can't get it even if you have.'

'No, I was on a tightrope with him though, almost toppling a few times but managed to keep it out of his nosey business.' Carl's breathing slowed. Paula and he kept silent until Beverly brought in the tea. Relating the entire evening's conversation he had had with Thomas he asked quite imploringly, 'What am I going to do about Joseph? They are spies; the pair of them. We have been taken for a long, long ride. I couldn't get the mother's address out of him. I've a good mind to call on the address we have but it's late. Tomorrow I will deal with Dora. I'm throwing her out, no questions asked.'

'I don't blame you,' said Beverly, laying the tray on the table.

'You can always bring young Joseph here for a bit,' offered Paula.

'No, I'm throwing Dora out.'

'Who will look after Joseph then?' asked Paula.

'Let me think about all this. I have to calm down a bit more.'

Beverly suggested that Joseph could live at Paula's home temporarily while Carl deals with Dora at a slower pace. Paula could get well rather quickly and then Beverly could move in with Carl when Dora has gone, to take care of Joseph.

'That's three people we have to deal with; the mother, Thomas and Dora,' said Carl.

'Thomas can hobble around on his own. We've been nothing but kind to him and for him to double cross everyone, well that's absolutely awful,' Beverly mused.

'We have to call the police and press charges against Thomas and his mother,' said Paula.

'Why?' Carl turned towards her a little confused.'

'Because of the illegal marriage to Beverly.'

'Of course; the illegal marriage. Well, let's do that right away.'

'I think we better get some advice first about all this,' said Beverly, 'let's just keep trying to calm down and once we've slept, you can sleep here Carl, we can…'

'No, better still,' said Carl, 'I'll go home and act as calmly as I can or Dora will panic and scarper, flee to her mother, they'll both flee then goodness knows where we'll find them. We don't know what Thomas will do or even what they might do to him.'

Paula sat pondering, brooding over an idea and then spoke up, 'The solicitor knows dad is dead now, he's got lots of evidence right there in the journal, the will and Thomas's birth certificate. Can't we let him deal with all this? We can carry on as normal and then spring the surprise on them all. We can make them think they are going to get away with everything. Thomas is at the sticky end so he can't run to his mother or Dora, physically or any other way. He'll think you are with Dora right now. He can phone her but he won't, what can he say?'

'That is pure wisdom, Paula, we should settle everything right down and in any case once the solicitor has read the journal he will be executing the will, won't he?'

'So that'll be the end of it. Yes, let's not take the matter into our own hands,' endorsed Carl. He stood to leave and thanked his sisters for their tolerance regarding his intrusion.

He drove home through the dark night feeling more relaxed. As for Dora, he would keep his peace but watch his mouth even more until the time was right. As he drew onto the driveway he tried to gather his thoughts but it was impossible. He turned off the ignition, snap; he had broken his relationship with Dora and would never turn it on again. Keep calm; try to be normal with her. He entered the hall, took off his coat and made his way to the kitchen. He breathed deeply while filling the kettle. He had to get to bed in a normal mood. As he sat on his own in the lounge, feet splayed wide over the carpet he wondered what he had done to deserve all this. What had any of them done to deserve it? He finished his hot chocolate, placed the mug in the kitchen sink, switched off the hall light, switched on the landing light and mounted the stairs. At the top he turned the knob to his son's bedroom, silently opened the door and bent down in the dark to kiss him goodnight. He kissed thin air. Turning quickly he switched on the light, no Joseph. He rushed into his bedroom, no Dora. Thomas! What have you done? When could this have happened? On his way to Paula's, Thomas thought he was on his way home and took his chance to warn Dora, it must be, but why when he had so much to lose?

Carl picked up the phone and called the police reporting the kidnapping then frantically called Beverly and Paula,

'Bring Paula over here with you Beverly right away, please. Dora has run off with Joseph, I'll explain when you get here.'

'Okay, Carl, we'll be over as soon as we can.'

Beverly sped to Paula's room. Both sisters rapidly dressed and shot down the stairs and to Beverly's car. Once at Carl's they found a police car outside. They knocked, Carl let them in.

The police were just leaving. 'Do either of you remember the address of Thomas's mother?' asked Carl.

'I do, will never forget it,' answered Beverly, 'it's, 71 Congress Road, Maidstone. Are you sure she'll be there, Carl.'

'Nowhere else she could be.'

❧

Alice opened the door to Dora and Joseph, who had been rudely awakened. He was crying and demanding loudly to be put back to bed.

'Where's Daddy?' he howled, 'I want Daddy.'

'Shut up boy,' snarled Alice, 'get in here and keep quiet or I'll put you in a cupboard and lock the door.'

Joseph's tears dried up immediately.

'Where can I put him?' Dora asked her aunt.

'Just lay him there a minute, on the couch. What did Thomas say to you?'

'He said he told Carl about me being your niece and that Carl knows everything but nothing about a journal and he told me Carl was on his way home to deal with me, whatever that meant.'

'Pretty obvious, how has he got to know everything if he hasn't got the journal?

'Thomas told him, I reckon, how else?'

'Thomas is no son of mine and no cousin of yours, got it? He's a traitor!' she shouted.

'Yes.' Dora stepped back in fear.

'Right, we are going to pay our pathetic Thomas a visit. He can't escape. Come on, get in the car.'

Dora reached down for Joseph.

Alice snapped, 'No, leave him. We won't be that long and he can sleep there or he'll just squeal and cry and hold us up.'

'We can't leave him.'

'Leave him!' Alice forcefully pushed her face towards Dora's.

'Okay,' Dora glanced at her son. He had fallen asleep, or pretended to.

Alice whipped her coat off the hook in the hall, grabbed Dora by the hand and pulled her out of the house.

'In the car and don't say anything at all to Thomas, I'll do the talking but do whatever I tell you.'

Dora remained silent. The journey with her aunt remained far from pleasant. She wished she was still at home and in bed. Had she over reacted? What if Thomas made everything up?

♋

The police had enough time to sound the siren. It would not be allowed after eleven. Joseph opened his eyes as blue lights flashed outside, behind the lounge curtains. He sat up then crept to the door. Two policemen approached and one of them rang the bell. Nobody answered. Joseph stood silently shaking with terror. The police opened the letter box then peered through to scan the hall. 'There's the little boy, standing right there.' the shorter one told the other. He looked back through the letter box. The boy was gone. They knocked once more then shouted through the letter box, 'It's okay Joseph, we are policemen and have come to take you back home to your daddy. Come to the door.

We are not going to hurt you.' Joseph slowly made his way back into the hall from the kitchen where he had hidden himself.

'Can you open the door and let us in?'

'I can't reach, I'm too small and I'm cold.'

'Can you see a chair to pull and stand on?'

'No.'

'Go and look in the kitchen or something and see what you can find.'

Joseph dragged one of the kitchen chairs along the hall, placed it near the lock and opened the door an inch.

'That's right, young lad, jump down and pull the chair away.'

Joseph pulled the chair away but left the door alone. The shorter policeman pushed it wider. Joseph stood, feeling lost and frightened.

The shorter policemen reached out towards the little fair haired lad and carried him to their car while the other closed the door and radioed the police station to say they had found the boy but no adults.

'Roger, take him home and question his father about where they could have gone.'

The shorter policeman told Joseph his name was James and sat in the back of the police car with him playing I Spy until they arrived at his house.

Carl opened the front door to them, 'Thank God,' he gasped with tears in his eyes. He took hold of Joseph gently and held him close for a while before asking Beverly to put him to bed.

'Where do you think they may have gone?' questioned one of the policemen, 'give me all addresses you know starting with Thomas's.

'I doubt they are with Thomas, as he is in hot trouble with his mother, at least he tells me that, unless…'

The taller policeman reached for his radio giving the addresses, which included Father O'Reilly's, to the squad car patrol who had already left the station.

'Roger, we are not that far from the premises now, over.' They announced ten minutes later. Have another car go to the priest, over.'

'Roger.'

The police at Carl's house stayed with them while the two other cars continued their journey to the respective homes.

'Hello, no sirens please, you don't want to let them know you are coming if they are on their way to Thomas's or even if they are there, over.'

'Roger.'

Carl's household waited in trepidation. The crackling radio remained open so they could hear updates as they came in.

'There's nobody at the priest's house, over.'

'Stay there and keep out of sight in case they do turn up, over.'

'Have you reached Thomas's yet? over.'

'Just about. We have parked the car in the lane… on our way up the drive… there's two cars at the end in front of the front window…over.'

'Okay we have them,' one policeman told Carl.

'Be careful, if she's there she's a real bad lady,' warned Carl.

'We will. Is there a back door?'

'Yes.'

'There is a back door so you may want to watch for that, they may try to escape. over.'

'The garden is fenced off, they can't run anywhere,' explained Beverly.

'It's okay stay at the front door, over.'

As the police neared the front door they heard a kafuffle going on inside. 'Shh,' the policemen motioned to one another, holding their warrants of arrest and a set of handcuffs each. The shorter policeman pressed the silver letter box open. Two women were physically attacking a man with brute force. Thomas's countenance bulged as he murderously fought back.

'We better get in.' Both policemen banged hard on the door. 'Police, open the door.'

'Help!' shouted Thomas.

'He wants help?' the shorter policeman mocked.

Alice scrambled to shove all she could in front of the door. Dora simply stood to attention. Both policemen shouldered the door which gave way after few lurches but with only an inch maneuvering space, they could not enter.

'You are all under arrest, anything you say will be taken down and used in evidence in a court of law. Call for backup, over.'

'Roger.'

'We need more men, get round here as soon as you can, over'

As soon as the backup arrived all four policemen shouldered the front door but more furniture had been shoved against it.

'Break the window, that's the only way. That one there, you'll never get in those small leaded lights.'

One by one the police entered the smashed window and after a chase upstairs Alice was cornered in Thomas and Beverly's bedroom. Two policemen had already handcuffed Thomas and Dora.

'What have we done?' Thomas asked.

'What have you done?' the policeman replied, aghast. 'We are arresting you for kidnapping, attempted murder, illegal marriage and resisting arrest.'

'I haven't attempted murder,' Thomas smugly replied.

'No matter, you are all guilty one way or the other.'

The older policeman commanded two to stay with the criminals while he and another one cleared a pathway in the hall.

'We'll have to board up that window, call the station and arrange it please.'

Once cleared, and after securing the house, they escorted the prisoners to the awaiting cars, separating them; Alice in one car and Thomas and Dora in the other.

Alice protested loudly, 'You don't understand. You haven't asked any questions. Don't you see it's all a set up? I've been set up by Thomas.' She turned in the other car's direction frothing with rage. 'I need to go home. I need my belongings.'

'You can tell us what we don't understand down at the station,' instructed the driver.

'Anything you say is being written down in evidence,' reminded the police officer she was handcuffed to. As they neared the end of the drive Alice glanced back again.

'Thomas will pay for this,' was the last thing she said before falling silent.

The police radio at Carl's house continued to relay messages to the police officer in attendance who addressed Carl, 'They are safely being taken to the station, you can enjoy a good meal now.'

'Well, thank God this has been short but it feels like an eternity. It's been anything but sweet,' said Carl.

The policemen shook hands with everybody and left the premises.

Beverly and Paula found comfortable chairs while Carl prepared a snack for everyone. With Joseph wrapped up in bed, they ate until satisfied, 'Would you like us to stay the night, Carl?'

'Please stay, yes, Beverly. You both can wear Dora's nightclothes. Until the will is read I will not be happy. That woman will surely try to work or think her way out of all this.'

'That's the nature of humans. To get out of trouble they have created for themselves. I hope Joseph will be able to forget about the incident and that it leaves no bad effects on him. I'm sure he'll be as right as rain tomorrow.' Beverly folded her arms, smiled while lifting her eyes to the ceiling and declared, 'we'll all be rejoicing tomorrow but still be wondering what on earth hit us.'

Carl blew the steam of his tea away into the cool air then took a sip. On his right Paula rested her eyes while listening to Carl and Beverly carry on talking, 'Tomorrow is a new day and a brand new life,' said Carl, 'but it still isn't over, not until we are well settled into our new circumstances. Can you phone the solicitor tomorrow Beverly? See if he has got on any further with the reading and everything.'

'Just as soon as it's nine o'clock. We don't have to pretend Paula is ill any more. We need to go and talk to Father O'Reilly in case he gets wind of the events of tonight. He's bound to realize. The police were there weren't they? He's probably been round to Paula's place or at least tried to phone. I think I'll ask Paula to come to my house tomorrow to see what has to be done, and of course we need to finish sorting dad's house. It's all taking far longer than we planned.'

'Yes, you never know what else you will find in that forsaken house,' said Carl, somewhat sarcastically.'

They gathered themselves together and left for bed, leaving everything to wash up in the morning.

The night passed without further incident.

On rising Beverly woke and cared for Joseph. 'Where's Mummy?' he asked as soon as she entered his room. Beverly had lain awake perusing the question before falling asleep in the early hours and had a ready answer,

'Mummy had to help somebody last night and she won't be back until the person is okay.' Joseph's proud smile set his day in a positive direction. After a hearty breakfast Carl left for work and Beverly drove Joseph to school then drove Paula back to her flat. After a little while both sisters left to see what they could do at Beverly's home. Before they left Beverly picked up the phone and dialed the solicitor's number not expecting news one way or the other.

'Hello, Mr Watlingstone?'

'Yes, speaking.'

'It's Mrs Springfield, Beverly Springfield. I came in last week.'

'I remember. I have read all your papers, journal included. Is it possible you can drop in to see me, say on Wednesday?'

'There's been an incident over here, Mr Watlingstone. It may make some difference to our case.'

'Oh, what's that?'

'Now that you have read everything you will know what I am talking about. All three have been arrested, that is; Alice Springfield, Dora Hopkins and Thomas, my husband.'

'That was quick work but why Dora?'

Beverly explained the details and asked if Paula could join her on Wednesday.

'By all means. It's good to have a witness and support.'

'She's been a great support so far and, yes, that is something of great value.'

'What time will suit you?' enquired Mr Watlingstone.

'From mid morning will do fine.'

'Can Carl make it as well? I'd like to execute the will.'

'Execute it? You are the executor?'

'Indeed I am, Ma'am.'

'Hold on a minute,' Beverly cupped her hand over the receiver, turned to Paula who sat opposite her picturesque fields on the settee but sideways, facing Beverly. 'He wants to execute the will on Wednesday.'

'Yeah? Wow, that's okay with me.'

Beverly lifted her hand from the receiver and gave the go-ahead.

'I'll phone Carl and our other brother Sidney, they are sure to be able to come. If not we can arrange a date as soon as possible. I'll confirm it before the days out.'

'That's fine, I'm here all day till five.'

Beverly replaced the receiver and clapped in excitement. Paula gazed across to the horizon, 'There *is* a horizon, Beverly; it's at the end of the fields. Dad could not see one except at sea.' A tear rose from a sense of joy mingled with compassion for her father. 'To think, all his life he waited for this moment, this very moment. I wonder if he can see us at all?' she swallowed, 'we must honour his memory somehow.'

'Yes, we must.'

'Tea before we go?'

'Yes, we can have it here. I won't want to stay at my house for too long.'

As Paula entered the kitchen the phone rang. Beverly answered and after a five minute conversation she returned the receiver to its rack. Paula brought the tea.

188

'Well, that was a Chief Inspector Morgan. He wants us to go down to the station to make a statement. So that's more stuff we have to do. It's a good job you pretended to be sick all this time and I'm looking after you or we'd never get the time.'

'Does he want us now?'

'Straight away but let's drink this first.'

They drank as quickly as possible before hurriedly exiting the flat and charging down to the station. On arrival Carl was just leaving.

'Oh Carl,' Beverly called, 'the solicitor wants to execute the will. Can you come down on Wednesday? About mid morning? Eleven - ish?'

Carl halted and stepped closer to his sisters, 'I'm sure I can get out of work. Ring me to confirm the time.'

'Okay, Oh, I almost forgot, I will pick up Joseph at three from school and stay at your house till you get home; so much to do.'

'And phone Sidney or would you like me to?' reminded Carl.

'Please would you do that? We have so much on.'

'All the best in there.' Carl disappeared round the corner.

It took Beverly and Paula a couple of hours to finish their statements which were taken in separate rooms. On meeting up with Paula later Beverly asked,

'Did the police ask if they could see the journal and everything?'

'Yes, but I said it was up to the solicitor and Carl.'

'Oh, okay. They'll need to anyway to make their cases up, I suppose. They told me Thomas was pretty well shaken up, bleeding quite badly on his chin and bruised all over. They were trying to kill him, you know.'

'I know, that's awful.'

'He's in hospital but when he comes out it's straight back in the nick with him.'

'Yes, I've pressed charges for his illegal marriage. He helped get Joseph kidnapped and in no uncertain terms I don't want him back.'

'I wonder what Carl said about him.'

'That's anybody's guess. I'm sure he'll tell us later.'

'Let's get some lunch at my house.'

The two of them journeyed in silence, both pretty tired.

'Home, sweet home,' said Beverly, 'Man, look at that window. It's a good job that one was there or they'd never have got in.' Once in the house they could barely move for the amount of furniture that had been scattered all over the hall. 'We'll have it fixed up in no time,' laughed Beverly. The nurses, with hearts knit together spruced up the house, phoned for the glazier to fix the window and discussed where Beverly would live now that Thomas had been arrested. Paula suggested she live with her. Dora would surely be convicted alongside Alice for her part in assaulting Thomas. Either way Carl would not permit her into the house again. She was a traitor and a very good actress who would never be involved with her son again. 'As soon as dad's house is finished I'm packing my things and moving out,' announced Beverly, impulsively.

'It will be a real shame to lose this house but Thomas owns it so it's up to him, I suppose,' answered Paula.

'The only real thing I will miss is my shadow.'

'The true master of the house,' agreed Paula.

'And the most faithful; no truer a friend.'

They did not spend that long at the house. Beverly dropped Paula home so that she could pick up Joseph from school and together they waited for Carl to come home. Later she phoned Paula to ask if she was willing to spend the evening at their father's house to tie up loose ends and finish off sorting. 'Come round to Carl's for supper then we can go along together,' invited Beverly.

Beverly made herself busy cooking jacket potatoes and baked beans with grated cheese. It was Joseph's favourite and she must spoil him for a few days. The atmosphere was happy but Joseph's face always dropped not long after a laugh,

'Is Mummy coming home soon?'

Carl answered, 'Mummy is going to be away for a long time, Joseph, but Aunty Beverly and Aunty Paula are here to help while she is away. Be a good boy for them. We can play football on Saturday with some of your friends from school, would you like that?'

'Yes.'

'Well eat up and look lively, mate.'

Beverly reached out to ruffle Joseph's hair. His adorable smile moved her heart; at least she would get to know her nephew now.

'You two get going,' ordered Carl, 'I will wash the pots and Joseph will help, won't you, Joseph?' Joseph simply nodded.

On the way the sisters kept quiet while each dreamt about what change they would be confronted with in the following hours. At their father's house both of them marched upstairs in single file. They finished sorting their old bedrooms and the airing cupboard. 'Let's just get the entire place done tonight then we can relax for good,' suggested Beverly.

Next to sort was the library itself at the foot of their father's bed. Beverly pulled out one book at a time. Paula flicked through each one. It was a habit she had developed since she first threw any book out to make sure no bookmarks or notes were left inside. It was when they came to the Bible that she stopped to take her time. 'This is priceless,' she told Beverly, 'we didn't read it, did we? It's almost brand new. What is it about the Bible that people cherish so much that they don't even open it's pages? It's not exactly like a bone china tea set that could break easily. If handled properly it will last forever.' Beverly's face remained passive. 'I prayed twice and twice something significant happened. Maybe we should pray more?' Paula studied the titles of the books inside, 'I will read this from cover to cover soon.'

'I might join you.'

'Maybe we should have one each?'

'You keep that one then and I'll buy one. You asked for it, Paula.' They filled four boxes with the books, labeling them as they went and, once finished, pulled the cream painted plywood library out of its place.

'What's this, Paula?'

'What?'

'This,' Beverly pointed to a one foot square shaped door behind the library.

'Let's see, it's got a hole, pull it with your finger, see what happens.'

Beverly put her left forefinger inside and gave a tug. The door opened easily, she looked inside. A single enveloped lay perpendicular to the left hand side. 'Yet another envelope. Dad surely kept stuff, not much in here but let's see what's in it.' They sat on the bed. 'You open it Paula.' Paula took the envelope and tore the seam across the top. She opened it and offered the contents to Beverly. Beverly pulled out another thickly stuffed envelope and emptied the contents on the bed.

'These are receipts, hey, I remember in dad's journal he mentioned there were receipts under lock and key,' she said.

'Did he? I must have been dreaming, for what?'

'There's loads of them and cheque stubs. Help me with them, Paula.' As they opened one after the other they discovered that every item of furniture in Thomas's house belonged to their father, every single thing. There were other items missing, presumed sold or got rid of; figurines, Royal Crown Derby, crystal. Finally they unfolded the deeds of what looked like Alice's house and another, Thomas's house, all bearing their father's signature.

'Paula!'

'Beverly!'

'Let's put them all back. We need to get these to the solicitors at top speed. These are worth a fortune. It looks like dad has paid for everything belonging to Alice and Thomas,' Beverly squealed.

'Well, definitely Thomas, anyway. How could he afford all that?'

'Who knows but we're bound to find out. This is more than exciting.'

Beverly put all the receipts back into the envelope and handed it to Paula to put in her famous bag then left to celebrate by eating a superb roast lamb dinner at a local restaurant.

'At least you deserve it Paula, after all you've had to go through with flour on your face and everything.'

Paula laughed as she sipped her red wine, 'Would you like a sip?' she offered but Beverly declined even a hint of the alcohol.

'It would be a real shame if after all this I would get arrested for drink driving.'

'Quite.' Paula's flushed face amused Beverly, being more flushed than usual.

Beverly drove back to Paula's feeling like a contented child.

The following morning Beverly drove to Carl's with Paula to take Joseph to school. Without an appointment she drove Paula, together with the receipts, to the solicitor's. Mr Watlingstone took a step back when both women marched into his office. He had not yet settled to his day's work.

'We're so sorry just to barge in like this but we've found something of great interest.' Beverly handed over the package. Mr Watlingstone withdrew the small stubs and other fiddly bits of paper and glancing through them briefly invited them to sit down before declaring,

'Well, what a case you have! I will sort all this out as soon as possible and get back to you all with what I have come up with; hopefully at the end of the week. We'll cancel Wednesday's appointment to give me time.'

Beverly caught him up with the goings-on of the previous night. Paula wound her hair round her finger and pursed her lips. As she listened to her sister her thoughts turned again to her father. Beverly's voice seemed far away. Her father's tragic story sowed a completely different picture for his children. Joseph would not suffer like them. What he was experiencing regarding his mother could and would be forgotten. The family would pull together from now on to make sure of that and one day he too would know all about the sacrifice it took to deal with the villains of the family. He would not repeat any of it for his own children. Why did it take so long to heal a generation or even two? When Paula resurfaced from her mental wanderings Mr Watlingstone addressed her, 'Paula, you look far away. I was telling Beverly I will have everything sorted very soon and will read the will, all being well, at the end of the week. All this must be very upsetting and has surely turned your circumstances upside down.'

Paula answered, 'Yes but I'm glad it is all coming to an end now. The worst is over.'

Mr Watlingstone announced, 'I am hoping to let you know about a fortune of great proportions that will serve you all well for the future.'

All three stood, shook hands with each other and the sisters left the premises with their heads held high.

'Who tells Alice and Dora what he has found?' asked Paula as soon as they were out of earshot.

'I presume he does, or maybe the police will relay the news.'

'Crime certainly does not pay, Beverly, and we must make sure Joseph does not follow in his mother's footsteps. Living a double life is not worth it. I'm going to buy him a children's Bible so he can learn properly the difference between right and wrong.'

'Carl's a great dad. I'm sure he will be on the lookout for a new wife to care for Joseph.'

The sister's linked arms and disappeared round the corner to the waiting car.

'We'll be finished with dad's house today, for sure.'

As they headed back to the old council house, Beverly said, 'It's the end of an era, Paula.' She had already arranged for the house clearance company to remove all that was left. After a cup of tea and waiting another hour the van finally arrived. It took a couple of hours to empty the house completely. Finally, Beverly put her arm around Paula shoulder and both women strolled to the front door. Looking behind them Paula uttered a heartfelt prayer, 'Thank You for being with us and bringing so much good out of all this heartache.'

'And thank You for our dear father, Ralph Hopkins. I hope You are looking after him up there in Heaven,' Beverly added.

'Let's pick Joseph up, then when Carl gets home and after supper I will drive you home.'

Joseph began to settle down and getting used to his aunties he chattered quite freely. He thought often about his mother but not as seriously as he did at first. She was, after all, doing what she was supposed to be doing, somewhere else.

At supper the phone rang, Carl answered, 'Hello Father O'Reilly, what causes you to phone us? Is everything alright? Did the police turn up at your house the other night?' he fell silent while Father spoke, 'Ah you phoned Paula's but nobody answered.' He paused again; 'You want to speak to Beverly?' he looked towards the staring sisters. Beverly

194

nodded, 'She is right here, Father.' Again he kept silent, 'You wanted to tell us about a call you've had from Alice and Dora. Have they called you? Surely that's not allowed.' Carl hung his head as he listened, 'Alice has told you there is a will. I am aware there is a will but, Father, don't you listen to her and don't you speak to her or Dora, please. And Father, you forgot to tell the solicitor dad had died so this has held a lot up for us, but never mind it may all turn out for the better.' After pausing again he said, 'No need to apologize now, you know what happened the other night. Don't burden yourself with guilt, or I'll be hearing your confession instead of you mine. I know Alice and Dora are afraid of losing all they have gained, that's exactly right.' Another pause followed, 'Father we are having our supper right now, they are in custody, Thomas is in hospital and the will is to be read by the end of the week. All will be wrapped up by the weekend and we will be able to breathe easily once again.' He hung up the phone after saying bye.

'Didn't Father want to speak to me?' asked Beverly.

'Oh, I completely forgot. I'm sure if he didn't say anything to me that he wanted to talk to you about he will ring again.'

After their fish and chips supper, Joseph asked about his mummy,

'Has Mummy been naughty, Daddy?'

'You could say so, Joseph, just a bit but it isn't your fault.'

'Aunty Beverly told me…'

'Never mind, you don't really need to know. Mummy won't be coming home again for quite a long time but you have two lovely aunties who will take care of you.'

Joseph looked down at his plate, placed his knife and fork neatly in the middle and said, 'that's it then.' A tear landed on a batter crumb, 'I love Mummy.'

Carl stooped beside his son. Picking up his knife and fork he cut his fish, pierced it with the prongs of Joseph's fork and held it to his moist lips. 'I know you miss Mummy a lot, Joseph but if you don't eat up, we'll be missing you.'

'How?'

'Well, you'll become so skinny you'll slip down a drain outside. You won't want that and neither will we. And when Mummy comes home again, some time, she will want to find you fit and healthy, won't she?' It was the only thing Carl thought would placate his son but regretted taking on part of Thomas's lying character. One day he will have to explain.

Joseph smiled at the thought of being reunited with his mother, opened his mouth and encased the slightly greasy fish. 'It's cold.'

'Okay, eat it quickly before it gets any colder.' Carl smiled up at his sisters who suppressed a heavy flow of laughter.

'You are so wise,' giggled Beverly, trying to control herself.

As soon as they finished Beverly swept Joseph off his feet as he got down from the table. She, Carl and Paula kept him amused with a couple of his favourite games before putting him to bed. He had never had three people putting him to bed before but enjoyed it immensely. Beverly and Paula left for Paula's after he fell asleep. The following morning the same routine was applied to their new morning's activities.

Once back at Paula's, Beverly asked, 'We're not going to Mr Watlingstone's today are we? He's spending the extra time to make up our case. 'We better remind Carl to contact Sidney about the reading of the will tomorrow.'

Paula sat on the edge of her bed filing her nails. Staring down at them she advised that they dress in their best clothes and all go for a family meal afterwards.

'Who will look after Joseph?' asked Beverly.

'Carl could ask one of his teachers to take care of him until he picks him up. If it's three-ish we could pick him up. That is if Carl goes back to work following the reading.'

'Good idea. I better go around to my house to make sure everything is okay every day. You can come with me if you like, stay here or whatever.'

'I'll come, Beverly, at least until all this is over.'

'Thank you.'

Paula put her nail file away in the bedside locker. She glanced down at her father's precious Bible. Tomorrow she would start reading it. 'Alice and Dora, are probably both worrying about losing everything, well one thing is for sure. They have certainly gained a whole new life for themselves.'

'Exactly, it's a shame people don't think of the consequences before they embark on such treacherous behaviour against their own families, or those close to them.' Later in the afternoon after picking up Joseph from school and during supper Beverly asked Carl, 'Shall we all meet together somewhere in the morning?'

'Morning?'

'Yes, it's Friday, our big day.'

'Oh my goodness, I've completely forgotten to contact Sidney, better phone him right away.' After phoning he assured his sisters Sidney was well prepared for tomorrow. Mrs Feathergill had fussed around him to make sure he would look his best.

The following morning Beverly phoned Mr Watlingstone to confirm the time of the appointment then rang Carl at his work. Sidney turned up at Paula's on his bike at ten. His navy blue suit had weathered the ride well.

'Do I look alright?' he asked Beverly, once inside the flat.'

'You are absolutely brilliant, young man,' praised Beverly.

'Cup of tea before we go then?' offered Paula.

Beverly finished brushing her hair, 'If we have time it would be great.'

Sidney sat waiting for his sisters to join him. As they did so he wondered, 'What will we all be doing tomorrow?'

'It's anybody's guess, Sidney. Either way, it's going to be good.'

The three of them set off in Beverly's car to meet Carl who was waiting in the car park. They had arranged it the evening before. The siblings stepped from their vehicles, Beverly in her car with Paula and Sidney in Carl's.

'This is it. The grand entrance of the life of, I daren't say; a brand new life will be sufficient,' Carl said in anticipation.

'I am looking forward to this,' answered Paula. Beverly and Sidney agreed.

The foursome entered the building in order of age and made their way up to Mr Watlingstone's office. He had not opened the door as was his custom but had his secretary to do that job, just to play things down a bit.

'Good morning,' greeted Mr Watlingstone, 'do come in all of you and take a seat.'

'Thank you,' a chorus of voices answered.

'How about a cup of tea while we are dealing with this will and, other things?'

'That fine with us,' answered Beverly.

He called his secretary to make a pot.

'It's pay day for you too, Mr Watlingstone,' announced Carl.

Mr Watlingstone lowered his eyes and, dismissing the statement, brought out the file of Mr Ralph Hopkins from his cabinet.

'You all know…'

The secretary knocked, interrupting him, before wheeling the tea trolley into the room.

'Who is Carl?' Carl lifted his right hand. 'So, of course you are Sidney. You are a farm worker? Do you enjoy your work?'

'Yes, I do, thank you, very much so.'

'Right let's get down to business. The journal is by far of great family value and so you can take it home with you just as soon as we have finished with it and that goes for Thomas's birth certificate too.'

'I'll take care of those,' offered Beverly.

'Your father was a very sad man and he did his level best to do what was right. Everything was stacked against him. That woman deserves all she is getting now. I have spoken to the police and they say they have pressed charges against both Alice and Dora, Alice for being the instigator and Dora for being an accomplice, albeit unwittingly, she still followed but will get a lesser sentence.'

'I'm divorcing her straight away and Beverly needs to divorce Thomas just as soon.'

'We can start on that directly we finish this if you wish. Not today, of course, but later we will make appointments and we don't need to take up much time over those as we have all the evidence in front of us. We will need your marriage certificate just to confirm Dora's identity.'

'No problem,' replied Carl.

Mr Watlingstone proceeded to read the will but in paraphrase, 'Ralph, your father, had been granted part of a will from his mother Audrey and George Haines, who she later married. Audrey and George decided to save most of their earnings so that your father and his brothers would come into a generous inheritance. George met your grandmother when he moved into the area to run his greengrocer shop. He couldn't help noticing your Grandmother's sorry condition once she had let go of your father and uncles. He took pity on her and eventually won her over and married her. They saved a substantial amount and employed me as their solicitor also. Your father had inherited a double portion for the suffering his mother had caused him as a child but by the look of the receipts and the journal Alice has sideswiped most, if not all of it. If it was not for the receipts that Beverly and Paula had found there would be precious little left, that is, in comparison to what you will be getting. With Alice behind bars there is little she can do to contest anything. The four of you have been granted all that had been bought in Ralph's name: two houses and all their contents, all the money that Alice has in her accounts as her accounts were still in your father's name that amounted to £200,000. She had not yet changed them since his death; the cars that she and Thomas owned belong to you also. All that Alice and Dora have left are the clothes they stand up in. In everyday language and to make it simple I have cut out the legal talk but you are welcome to read it for yourselves if you wish. So there you have it.' The four siblings sat unable to respond. Mr Watlingstone did not wait but proceeded to say, 'As for my fees, I have waived every penny. Your father was a good friend of mine and so were his parents. In fact, what I have to tell you is that when your grandmother threw her boys out I happened to be one of them.'

'What,' they all gasped in unity.

'Yes, I changed my name by deed poll before I moved back into the area. I didn't want to be recognized by anyone who may remember my name. Just didn't want to take a chance. I took my new surname after

Watling Street. There's only one Watling Street so I made Watlingstone out of it.

'You are our brother?' asked Paula, shocked.

'No, I am your uncle, Uncle Arthur.'

'One of the twins! And you are not going to charge us a penny?'

'No, not a penny.'

'How very kind of you,' declared Sidney.

'And what's more I will be here for you whenever you need anything legal from me from now on, divorces next. Family is always free and will take priority but I will always judge fairly with whatever information I have before me.'

'Well, I'm totally numb, completely,' Carl said, 'Did dad and his mother and George know who they were dealing with?'

'Not at first. I told them in the end when they were about to pay. I let them off too but I swore them to secrecy and confidentiality. I must do the same with you. Word must not get outside of this room so make sure you do not talk about this in public anywhere.'

'Will you come and visit us. Can we be family?' asked Paula.

Mr Watlingstone replied, 'We are family but as for visiting, definitely, we could arrange certain get-togethers but again we will have to be discreet. When I read Ralph's journal I had a hard job to keep reading. I knew he was my brother the minute I read his name, Ralph Hopkins, but I still researched him to make sure.'

'What has happened to the rest of his brothers, do you know?' asked Beverly.

'Of course, hadn't the Salvation Army traced them concerning our mother's will?'

'How come they didn't contact Ralph?'

The Salvation Army contacts a person who is being traced and if they do not wish to be traced then they do not have to be found by whoever is tracing them. In your father's case, he answered by writing to them and regretfully informed them that though he wanted very much to be in touch with them circumstances would not allow it. If Alice had got wind of them I'm sure, well, I'm sure he was protecting them.

'Well, what of them now? Are they around? Can we contact them?'

Mr Watlingstone reached for his intercom and pressed the buzzer,

'Miss Hayward, can you bring the men up.'

'Right away, Sir.'

The siblings daren't even move their eyes to look at one another. All of them in their thirties remained children at heart. A knock on the door by Miss Hayward invited a hearty 'come in' from Mr Watlingstone. She opened the door. The six men entered all bearing gifts which they placed on Uncle Arthur's desk. With a desk his size there was plenty of room. Arthur introduced his nephews and nieces to them all in turn. The siblings were too shocked to respond immediately. Sidney stood first then the others followed suit to shake their hands.

'So now you see what I meant when I said, "I am hoping to let you know about a fortune of great proportions that will serve you all well in the future." My brothers and I, your uncles, will be very close to you from now on, if you would like that. There'll be no more Alices in your lives believe me, no more Doras and certainly no more Thomases.

The uncles presented each sibling with a gift from each of them. A rapid knock at the door startled the siblings. The uncle who stood nearest opened it, 'Ah wonderful,' he said, 'do come in Father O'Reilly.'

Father O'Reilly just about squeezed into the room, a beaming smile broke out over his bonny Irish face, 'May the Lord be praised,' he chanted before Carl queried,

'Father O'Reilly? How come you are here?'

'I...,' he started then Uncle Arthur took over,

'When you first contacted me I had to inform Father O'Reilly of the problem. I have been seeing him for quite a while, following your case more closely than I will reveal. It was Father O'Reilly that organized your other uncles to be the pall bearers.'

'The pall bearers,' exclaimed Beverly, 'that's where I've seen you before!'

Mr Watlingstone smiled before carrying on, 'and, of course, he didn't let anybody know what he was doing in case it didn't work out. Somehow the time didn't seem right but when you handed me the journal it all changed. We had to bring them in to meet you all. Father O'Reilly deserves all the thanks and honour for all he has done in bringing such awful events to the wonderful conclusion it is.'

Beverly stepped forward, 'Father O'Reilly how can we thank you enough? This must be a dream. Tomorrow we will all wake up and wonder that it has happened at all.'

With twelve people filling the room and such an air of victory prevailing, Carl announced, 'We were going to celebrate with a family meal. You must all come with us,' his face wet with tears, 'Boys don't cry, do they?' he managed, remembering the pain of his father's separation from his family. 'They do now.'

'It's all been organized,' said Uncle Arthur. 'I have arranged for no clients for the entire day, just to spend time with all of you. We will have a banquet.'

The siblings reached out to hug their uncles, Father O'Reilly and each other.

'You must come and meet Joseph sometime,' invited Carl, 'What he wouldn't do with seven grand uncles!'

The world that had tortured their struggling father bowed its head and surrendered.